Decolonised Minds: When Radical Becomes Rational

A Framework for Decolonising Psychotherapy
Talha AlAli

Decolonised Minds Press

Decolonised Minds: When Radical Becomes Rational. A Framework for Decolonising Psychotherapy

First Published by Decolonised Minds Press 2025

ISBN: 978-1-0681890-0-5 (pbk)

ISBN: 978-1-0681890-1-2 (hbk)

ISBN: 978-1-0681890-2-9 (ebk)

**DECOLONISED
MINDS PRESS**

DEDICATION

To my parents, who always saw my anger toward injustice and unjust situations as a healthy sign—one they nourished rather than punished.

To my older brothers, who taught me to think for myself instead of following them blindly.

To my younger sister and brother, who taught me that leadership comes not from might, but from light.

To my wife, who questions my certainties and gifts me deeper ways of being.

To my wife's family, who embraced me as their own in my diaspora.

To my little Sorcha Reem AlAli, the one who gave the energy to share this with the world—in the hope she grows up in a safer, less racist, and less misogynistic society.

To all those who gave me consent to tell their stories in this book, and to those who did not give their consent, yet still left me with life lasting learnings.

And to everyone who believes all human lives are equal.

Acknowledgments

To **Dr. Marguerite Woods**—thank you for your unwavering mentorship during the writing of this book. Your wisdom, patience, and belief in this work made the process not only possible, but deeply meaningful.

To **Mary Maher**, my clinical supervisor—thank you for holding space for reflection, growth, and challenge. Your presence and guidance helped me stay grounded and honest throughout my work in Ireland.

To **the friends and colleagues** who generously read drafts, shared insights, and offered honest feedback—your support shaped this book into what it needed to become.

To **every person** who has ever taught me—formally or informally—as teachers, lecturers, activists, trainees, or students: your lessons echo throughout these pages. I am forever learning.

I also honour **the communities** I have worked with—displaced, marginalised, and resisting—who have shown me what dignity and healing truly mean. This book is for you.

Finally, to **those walking the path of decolonising practice**: may this book be a companion in your courage and a mirror to your convictions.

Contents

"Decolonisation is always a violent phenomenon"

– Frantz Fanon

Introduction

Thank you for picking up this book. I mean that sincerely. There are many books on psychotherapy—thousands, in fact—and choosing this one means you are curious about something that too often remains unspoken in our field: the colonial foundations of psychological practice and the urgent need to decolonise them.

This book is self-published. That was a conscious decision. I chose not to submit it to a commercial publisher because I wanted full control over the pace, the tone, and the integrity of the content. I did not want it to be trimmed, neutralised, or restructured to make it more "palatable" to the very systems this book critiques. In other words, I did not want this work to be colonised on its way to publication.

But there is a price to this freedom. Without the support of a publishing house, marketing and visibility are major challenges. So, if you find this work useful—if it resonates with you, challenges you, or offers something valuable—please consider recommending it to your colleagues, students, supervisors, or institution. You are part of its journey now. And if you have any feedback, ideas for improvement, or even criticism, I would be genuinely grateful to receive it. You can reach me at **press@decolonised minds.ie**. My work is ongoing, and your input can help make it stronger.

Why This Book Matters

Decolonisation is not a metaphor, nor is it a checkbox. It is a political, personal, and psychological process. It is also messy, uncomfortable, and nonlinear. It asks us to look at what we have taken for granted—our training, our methods, our language, our sense of what "normal" looks like—and to examine whose stories and knowledge have been excluded.

For those of us who work in the field of mental health, this task is urgent. The tools we use were not created in a vacuum; they were shaped in specific cultural, historical, and political contexts. Many were developed in Europe and North America and then exported globally, often through colonial violence, missionary psychology, or international aid models that presumed their own universality. Today, these tools remain dominant in classrooms, clinics, and policy documents across the world. But dominance is not the same as truth. And universality is often a mask for erasure.

This book is not a rejection of all Western psychological knowledge. It is a call to put that knowledge into dialogue with other ways of knowing. It is a demand for balance, for plurality, and for justice.

What I Mean by Decolonisation

Decolonisation, as I define it in this book, is not a symbolic gesture or a substitute for diversity. It is a material, political, and psychological imperative. It involves the full recognition that colonised peoples have the right to repatriation, to reclaim the land, resources, and cultural knowledge that were violently taken or systematically erased. This includes restitution for historical and ongoing harm, as well as committed support for the restoration of languages, worldviews, and lifeways that colonisers actively sought to destroy.

In psychotherapy, decolonisation cannot be limited to multicultural inclusion or adjustments in language. It requires an active confrontation with the colonial logics that continue to govern our therapeutic frameworks—logics that privilege Western epistemologies, individualism, and pathologisation. Decolonising therapy means creating space for ancestral knowledge, collective memory, political consciousness, and community-defined forms of healing. It is not simply about adapting therapy to the client's culture; it is about transforming the assumptions that underpin what therapy is, who it serves, and whose truths it honours.

Decolonising Begins with Ourselves

One of the central ideas in this book is simple but difficult: we cannot begin to decolonise the minds of our clients if we have not first done that work ourselves. This means engaging in honest, sometimes painful reflection on how we have internalised colonial logics—logics of superiority, neutrality, individualism, and control. It means asking: Whose voices shaped our training? Whose suffering gets named and treated? Whose resilience gets overlooked or misunderstood?

Decolonisation is not just about the content of what we do in therapy; it is about the frameworks that guide how we think, listen, respond, and intervene. It is not something you add to your practice; it is a shift in how you understand the very purpose of the work.

Advocacy Without Superiority

This book is also written in the hope of clarifying some ethical boundaries around advocacy. Advocating for the rights of a group of people does not require you to agree with or even approve of all of their beliefs. Advocacy, when done ethically, is rooted in the recognition of shared humanity—not ideological conformity. When a marginalised community asks for dignity, safety, and voice, our support should not be conditional. Human rights are not earned by ideological alignment. They are inalienable.

At the same time, advocating for a group of people does not automatically make us their spokespersons. That role, if it is needed at all, should be granted by the community itself—not assumed by outsiders, even well-meaning ones. Solidarity does not require centre stage. Often, it requires stepping back, listening, and redirecting attention to the people most affected.

Finally, it is worth saying clearly: decolonising your practice does not make you superior to others. It should make your practice more ethical, but not to assume that you are more enlightened, or more evolved. The belief in superiority—whether based on race, class, religion, gender, or ideology—is one of the most enduring legacies of colonialism. If we replicate that belief in the name of decolonisation, we betray the very work we claim to do. Decolonisation requires humility, not heroism.

A Call to Collective Responsibility

This book is not only for therapists. It is for educators, supervisors, students, policymakers, and anyone who wants to think critically about the systems that shape mental health. Decolonising psychotherapy is not a solo project. It requires collective, institutional, and cultural change. It requires us to rethink how we train new therapists, how we write diagnostic manuals, how we allocate resources, how we define evidence, and how we honour lived experience.

Most importantly, **decolonising the minds of those we work with cannot happen unless we also commit to decolonising the minds of those who continue to benefit from colonial structures**. This includes the institutions we work in, the educational systems we uphold, and the inner frameworks we carry unconsciously. If we fail to engage with the minds of the colonisers—whether that means individuals or institutions—we risk reinforcing the very dynamics we hope to dismantle.

An Invitation, not a Blueprint

You will not find a single model or checklist in this book. That is by design. Decolonisation is not a method to be standardised; it is a conversation to be sustained. It is rooted in place, context, history, and relationship. What works in Palestine may not work in Ireland. What heals in Bangladesh may not translate in Ukraine. But what unites these contexts is the shared insistence that people must be seen, heard, and honoured in the fullness of their humanity.

Therefore, consider this book an invitation. An invitation to question what you know, to listen more deeply, to make space for discomfort, and to stay in the work even when it gets hard. Especially when it gets hard.

While this book is not a manual, it does follow a clear structure. The chapters are intended to build on each other, moving from historical foundations to clinical practice, through critique, reflection, and into action. Some chapters are more conceptual, others more practical. All are written with the same aim: to support a process of honest questioning, critical engagement, and meaningful change.

- **Chapter 1 – The Colonial Mind: Unpacking the Legacy of Oppression in Mental Health**: Looks at how colonialism shaped the foundations of psychology and psychiatry, and how these foundations continue to inform what is considered normal, disordered, treatable, or untreatable.

- **Chapter 2 – Trauma and the Colonised Mind**: Explores how trauma is experienced, expressed, and silenced in communities affected by colonisation, conflict, and displacement. Challenges the limits of Western trauma models and highlights the need for culturally grounded approaches.

- **Chapter 3 – The Foundations of a Decolonised Psychotherapy Practice**: Offers a starting point for thinking about what decolonised practice might actually involve. Focuses on power, positionality, humility, and the shift from therapist as expert to therapist as listener, witness, and collaborator.

- **Chapter 4 – Social Justice and Decolonised Psychotherapy**: Argues that psychotherapy is not politically neutral—and never has been. Looks at how therapy can either reinforce or challenge structural injustice, depending on how it is practised.

- **Chapter 5 – The Role of Resistance in Healing**: Centres resistance as a legitimate and often necessary response to oppression. Draws from clinical work, activism, and cultural traditions to show how resistance can be part of psychological survival and dignity.

- **Chapter 6 – Complex Intersections: Migration, Identity, and Decolonising Psychotherapy**: Examines how intersecting forms of oppression—racism, xenophobia, unchilding, religious targeting—impact marginalised people in therapy. Focuses especially on migrants, refugees, and displaced communities.

- **Chapter 7 – The Pluralistic Approach to Psychotherapy and Its Connection to Decolonised Psychotherapy**: Looks at the pluralistic model and asks what it has to offer— and where it can improve. Proposes ways to adapt pluralistic practice to better engage with decolonial thinking and non-Western knowledge.

- **Chapter 8 – Ethics, Boundaries, and Self-Reflexivity in Decolonised Psychotherapy**: Revisits ethical frameworks and questions some of the assumptions behind professional boundaries. Argues for relational, transparent, and culturally attuned forms of care that account for power and context.

- **Chapter 9 – Limitations of Decolonised Psychotherapy: Challenges and the Path Forward**: Offers a critical look at the risks of co-optation, superficial change, and institutional resistance. Reflects on the internal and external tensions that arise when trying to decolonise within systems that remain fundamentally colonial.

- **Chapter 10 – Imagining the Decolonised Future: Transformation, Action, and Collective Healing**: Brings the threads together. Outlines practical steps for change, while acknowledging that the work will always be unfinished. Asks what it would mean to take decolonisation seriously—not as a metaphor, but as an ongoing commitment.

You may not agree with everything in these pages. That is fine. This work is not about agreement. It is about reflection, responsibility, and reparation.

Thank you for being here. Thank you for reading with an open mind and heart. And thank you, in advance, for being part of what comes next.

Chapter One

The Colonial Mind

Unpacking the Legacy of Oppression in Mental Health

"*Exile is strangely compelling to think about but terrible to experience. It is the unhealable rift forced between a human being and a native place, between the self and its true home: its essential sadness can never be surmounted. And while it is true that literature and history contain heroic, romantic, glorious, even triumphant episodes in an exile's life, these are no more than efforts meant to overcome the crippling sorrow of estrangement.*"
— Edward Said, Reflections on Exile

Decolonisation is more than an academic discourse or political aspiration—it is the radical act of remembering what was buried, recovering what was distorted, and restoring what was deliberately denied. It is the process of tending to the wounds of exile, displacement, and cultural erasure. It is a reclamation of identity, spirit, and memory. Colonisation was never solely about territory; it was equally about the colonisation of the mind. The imposition of foreign systems of governance was accompanied by the implantation of foreign systems of thought, seeking to reconfigure how individuals perceived themselves, their communities, and the world around them (Fanon, 1963; Ndlovu-Gatsheni, 2013)

This mental occupation continues to haunt us. It lingers in the foundational assumptions of psychology, psychiatry, and therapeutic practice. Today's global mental health systems are still structured by Eurocentric epistemologies—ways of knowing that marginalise, distort, or pathologise the worldviews of colonised peoples (Fernando, 2017; Kirmayer & Swartz, 2014).

To begin any trauma-informed journey through psychotherapy, one must first confront this historical legacy. For how can we foster genuine healing without first identifying the root of the harm? Decolonisation does not end with dismantling; it requires a simultaneous act of remembrance and renewal. It asks us to hold oppressive systems accountable while also holding ourselves accountable; to the stories, traditions, and lifeways that colonialism tried to erase but could never fully extinguish. These remnants are not just ruins; they are seeds, waiting for conditions in which they can grow again (Smith, 2012; Watkins & Shulman, 2008).

In psychotherapy, decolonisation begins with recognising that many of the tools we use—diagnostic systems, therapeutic techniques, even the structure of the therapy room—were developed within Western cultural and philosophical traditions that exclude vast portions of the human experience (Summerfield, 2008). These models often exported globally as neutral or universal, in fact reflect the concerns, values, and priorities of white, individualistic, industrialised societies (Henrich, Heine, & Norenzayan, 2010). What becomes pathologised in one culture may be sacred in another. What is labelled "disorder" may, elsewhere, be understood as relational disconnection, spiritual crisis, or ancestral calling.

Thus, radical unlearning is essential. Decolonising psychotherapy means peeling back the layers of Eurocentric bias embedded in everything from psychometric instruments to cognitive behavioural protocols. It does not necessarily mean rejecting Western psychology in its entirety, but recontextualising it—decentring it as the default authority and creating space for Indigenous, African, Middle Eastern, Asian, and diasporic psychologies to stand as co-equals (Kessi, 2020; Moodley & Palmer, 2006).

A useful metaphor is that of rewilding: restoring a forest to its natural, unmanicured state so that diversity can return. Likewise, decolonised psychotherapy seeks to rewild the psychological landscape—to create room for multiplicity, contradiction, and cultural specificity. It acknowledges that no single model or tradition can claim universality, and that healing often lies in the spaces where different systems meet and are held in respectful dialogue. This pluralistic ethos resonates strongly with the Pluralistic Approach developed by John McLeod and Mick Cooper (2012), which this book returns to in Chapter 7. Their framework emphasises collaboration, client agency, and methodological flexibility—values that align closely with decolonised ethics, though the two are not synonymous.

Psychiatry's historical entanglement with colonialism deserves particular scrutiny. In many colonial contexts, psychiatry was not a healing science but a mechanism of control—used to pathologies resistance, enforce obedience, and erase cultural expression. Frantz Fanon, the revolutionary psychiatrist and anti-colonial thinker, explored this dynamic in *The Wretched of the Earth* (1963). He argued that colonial psychiatry treated the colonised as inherently deficient—morally, intellectually, and emotionally—and that psychiatric institutions in colonised nations became instruments of subjugation. In French-occupied Algeria, for example, psychiatric hospitals served as holding centres for those deemed politically disruptive or psychologically deviant—categories often indistinguishable in the eyes of the colonisers (Fanon, 1963; Keller, 2007).

Spiritual practices, communal rituals, and ancestral healing systems were dismissed as "superstition," "witchcraft," or "madness." Indigenous peoples were alienated not only from their land, but from their cosmologies and healing traditions—cut off from the languages and lineages that once anchored their sense of self and wellbeing (Adams, 2020; Kirmayer et al., 2003). These ruptures were not incidental; they were central to the colonial project. They continue to echo in the ways that mainstream psychology too often dismisses non-Western idioms of distress and culturally grounded coping strategies.

Western Psychiatry as a Gatekeeper of Healing

Today, the dominance of Western diagnostic frameworks such as the Diagnostic and Statistical Manual of Mental Disorders (DSM) and the International Classification of Diseases (ICD) continue to shape global mental health practice. These manuals, though significant in standardising psychiatric care, often carry the unacknowledged legacies of colonial epistemologies. They are not neutral tools; they are rooted in a particular worldview—one that prioritises individualism, pathology, and biomedical objectivity, often at the expense of cultural meaning and collective context (Fernando, 2010; Summerfield, 2008).

Behaviours that may be interpreted as spiritual devotion, ancestral connection, or communal mourning in one culture are too often pathologised under these diagnostic systems. Ecstatic ritual becomes mania; prolonged grief becomes major depression; dreams of departed ancestors are deemed hallucinations. In their pursuit of scientific legitimacy, these frameworks flatten the nuanced textures of human experience into rigid taxonomies (Kirmayer et al., 2014; Watters, 2010). This is not simply a technical problem—it is a deeply ethical one. Who decides what constitutes "illness," and on whose terms is recovery defined?

After centuries of brutal colonisation, genocide, cultural erasure, and forced assimilation, Western governments and institutions now extend their power by prescribing the frameworks through which colonised peoples must pursue healing. The violence of colonisation continues through this clinical paternalism: colonised nations are told not only how they were broken, but how they must mend. Unless healing aligns with Western psychiatric standards, it is often dismissed or excluded. This shift from territorial domination to psychological governance reveals the deeper function of mental health systems in postcolonial contexts. Psychiatry, in this form, becomes less about healing and more about regulating legibility—deciding whose suffering counts, whose recovery is valid, and whose cultural knowledge can be trusted (Kessi, 2020; Mills, 2014).

Working from a decolonised lens requires a different starting point. Instead of asking, "What disorder fits this person?", the therapist asks, "What does this person's suffering mean in the context of their culture, their community, their history, and their story?" This shift is not cosmetic—it is transformative. It moves the centre of gravity from pathology to possibility, from diagnosis to dialogue, from expertise to mutual recognition. The decolonised therapist does not claim to fix, but rather to witness, to hold, and to co-create the conditions for meaning to emerge (Freire, 1970; Watkins & Shulman, 2008).

Listening, however, is not passive. It demands humility and the courage to admit uncertainty. It requires that the therapist release the role of the infallible expert and become a companion—present, reflexive, and porous to other ways of knowing. This process of humility is not one of loss, but of liberation. It makes space for something richer: the possibility of truly meeting clients where they are, rather than where the profession expects them to be.

Cultural Amnesia, Trauma, and the Legacy of Double Consciousness

Trauma, in Western psychology, is often framed as an individual rupture—an event that disturbs the integrity of the self. But in many Indigenous, African, Middle Eastern, and diasporic traditions, trauma is seen as communal, intergenerational, and ecological. It is not merely lodged in the brain or body, but carried in family stories, in rituals, in collective silence, and in the land itself (Atkinson, 2002; Kirmayer, Gone, & Moses, 2014). To confine healing to the individual is to misunderstand the very nature of the wound.

Colonisation not only dispossessed peoples of land—it dislocated them from their identities. Languages were criminalised, spiritualities demonised, histories erased. The sociologist W.E.B. Du Bois (1903) famously captured this internal fracture as "double consciousness"—the condition of seeing oneself through the eyes of a society that devalues one's origins. This conflict creates a psychic wound that cannot be traced to a single traumatic event, but to centuries of cultural violence. It is the ache of belonging nowhere, of measuring oneself against imposed ideals of civility, sanity, and worth.

For many in formerly colonised communities, this wound manifests as intergenerational trauma—not only psychologically, but biologically. Emerging research in epigenetics supports what many cultures have long intuited: trauma can be inherited, passed down through stress responses encoded in DNA (Yehuda et al., 2015). But while science may now validate these truths, many colonised people have long carried them without recognition.

Another legacy of colonial domination is the erosion of trust in traditional systems of healing. When spiritual practices and ancestral medicine are cast as primitive or unscientific, generations are taught to mistrust their own tools. Even when these practices survive colonisation, they are often reclaimed with uncertainty, as if their legitimacy depends on Western approval. This produces a form of cultural self-doubt—a silencing of the very voices that once sustained resilience. Meanwhile, Western psychology begins to appropriate these same practices—mindfulness, ritual, storytelling—without accountability to their origins.

In this context, decolonising therapy is not a luxury or trend; it is a necessity. It is a political, ethical, and spiritual act—an act of rehumanisation for both therapist and client. As Du Bois, Fanon, and others remind us, liberation is not only structural—it is psychic. And to engage in this work is to begin healing wounds that were never meant to be seen, let alone named.

Restoring Severed Roots: A Personal Reflection

People who have been cut off from their cultural and ancestral roots may adapt to new places and cultures. They may succeed in life, speak new languages, navigate new systems, even rise within them—but something essential can still be missing: a connection to the past, to the wisdom and resilience of those who came before. Decolonised psychotherapy seeks to restore those severed roots, to offer not only understanding but reconnection—to memory, to community, to a sense of meaning beyond survival.

This work is not abstract or theoretical. It is deeply personal. As a psychotherapist whose journey has been shaped by the intersections of culture, religion, identity, trauma, and historically disadvantaged skin colour, I have lived the impacts of colonial legacies. Growing up in a part of the world where empire's fingerprints remain etched into institutions, borders, and daily life, I witnessed how these legacies silence voices, distort self-perception, and create invisible ceilings. I know how they can infiltrate the psyche, forcing one to question their worth and legitimacy. But I have also seen—within myself and others—how these legacies can be named, challenged, and slowly transformed.

In this journey, storytelling becomes more than narrative—it becomes medicine. In many cultures, storytelling is how knowledge is passed on, how memory survives when institutions forget, and how identity endures in exile. Stories are not simply words; they are carriers of belonging. They remind us that our wounds are not isolated, and that our lives are linked to those who came before and those who will come after. In a decolonised therapeutic space, stories create bridges—between past and present, between individual and collective, between pain and the possibility of healing (Archibald, 2008; Denborough, 2008).

But storytelling is not enough. It must be joined with action—with a commitment to restructure the systems that perpetuate disconnection. Decolonisation does not stop at uprooting the weeds of colonialism; it also involves tending to the garden that remains. It means creating an environment where diverse forms of healing can coexist. Where no one tradition claims superiority. Where CBT and indigenous cosmologies can exist side by side—not as opposites, but as co-conspirators in the work of care.

In practical terms, this means developing therapeutic practices that resonate with clients' lived realities. It means designing therapy rooms that reflect the communities they serve, integrating rituals, languages, symbols, and values that hold meaning. It means collaborating with elders, cultural leaders, and grassroots healers. And it means constantly listening—to the wisdom that was once called primitive, to the knowledge that has been waiting to return, and to the people whose voices were buried beneath colonial rubble.

One of the many lessons I have learned in this work is that decolonisation is never linear. It is layered, emotional, at times profoundly disorienting. It demands discomfort, and it resists shortcuts. I have come to better understand why Fanon said, "Decolonisation is always a violent phenomenon." Not always in the literal sense—but in its disruption of narratives, institutions, and comforts. It means standing in the liminal space where histories collide and futures are rewritten. It means holding the personal and the political in the same breath. It means looking at inherited wounds—not to be paralysed by them, but to refuse their invisibility.

In my work as a therapist, I have met clients whose struggles with anxiety, low self-worth, and fractured identity are not reducible to isolated experiences or chemical imbalances. Their distress often finds its roots in narratives imposed across generations—narratives of inferiority, alienation, and erasure, birthed in the colonial project. These narratives did not simply discredit their ancestors' knowledge; they replaced it with emptiness, with a manufactured silence that tells them they are not enough. The task of decolonised psychotherapy is to meet these stories not with diagnosis, but with deep listening and truth-telling, to help individuals remember who they were before they were told to forget.

To truly decolonise the mind, we must first recognise that colonialism was not only an act of violence against bodies—it was an act of violence against stories. Edward Said, in his seminal work Culture and Imperialism (1993), captures this truth when he argues that imperialism constructs cultural narratives that frame the colonised as inferior, incomplete, or uncivilised without Western intervention. Said's analysis offers a powerful lens through which to understand the psychology of colonisation: the more pervasive the narrative of inferiority, the more deeply it becomes embedded in the psyche of the colonised.

In psychotherapy, these narratives appear in forms that seem mundane but are profoundly significant—a young woman ashamed of her accent, a man suppressing his grief because he has been taught that vulnerability is weakness, or a child who hides their heritage out of fear of ridicule. Drawing from Said's critique of colonial narrative power, I believe that healing cannot end with deconstruction. It must also involve reconstruction—a deliberate act of creating or reclaiming stories that affirm complexity, dignity, and cultural integrity. It is not enough to critique the soil; we must plant something new within it.

One client I worked with carried a heavy burden of intergenerational trauma. His family had experienced forced displacement, like many whose lands were seized by colonial powers. He grew up hearing his grandparents' stories—stories that were drenched in suffering, loss, and longing. His identity became entangled with their trauma. He felt that he had inherited only pain. But together, in the therapy room, we looked again. We re-examined the same stories through another lens—the resilience embedded in them, the creativity of rebuilding life in exile, the cultural practices that had survived oceans and silence. Slowly, he began to see himself not only as the bearer of trauma but as the inheritor of strength. As he re-authored these intergenerational narratives, I often thought of Fanon's words: "Each generation must, out of relative obscurity, discover its mission, fulfil it, or betray it." Fanon spoke of decolonisation as a revolutionary act, and I agree. To decolonise is to reclaim the right to narrate one's own story. It is to refuse the confines that others have drawn and to choose instead a fuller, richer map of the self.

This reclamation is where trauma-informed care becomes vital. When we confront the psychological wounds left by colonialism—racism, cultural erasure, spiritual invalidation—we must begin with safety. Trauma is not only what happened to someone; it is how their nervous system learned to survive in response. Clients navigating the lifelong effects of oppression often carry an understandable mistrust—not just toward others, but toward themselves. They may doubt their own instincts, struggle to believe their pain is real, or feel ashamed of their emotions, because those very things have been dismissed by the world around them.

Trauma-informed therapy offers a way back. Not just a way back into the therapeutic relationship, but a way back into self-trust. When I began to integrate culturally grounded, trauma-informed practices into my work, I was struck by how many healing traditions from Indigenous and non-Western cultures already embodied these principles. Communal rituals, ceremony, embodied movement, and storytelling—these practices create safety, recognise the sacredness of emotion, and affirm relational interdependence. These are not new inventions; they are long-held wisdoms that have simply been marginalised by Western clinical dominance (Archibald, 2008; Gone, 2013). To decolonise psychotherapy is not to supplement Western models with cultural "add-ons"—it is to honour the epistemologies that preceded them and continue to flourish, often in resistance.

Land plays a critical role in this reconnection. For many cultures, the land is not just a physical place—it is memory, identity, spirit, and ancestor.

In Arabic, the phrase "the land is the honour" expresses this sacred bond. Colonialism shattered these relationships, turning sacred landscapes into commodities and their stewards into displaced labour. In therapy, I have seen how returning to the land—even in symbolic or sensory ways—can trigger deep healing. A walk in a forest. Planting a seed. Placing one's hands in soil. These acts become ceremonies of remembrance. As Māori scholar Linda Tuhiwai Smith (2012) writes, "The land remembers what has been forgotten." And in that remembering, we too may find pieces of ourselves that were once lost.

But decolonisation is not nostalgia. It is not a return to an imagined past where everything was pure or perfect. It is a weaving—of old and new, of rupture and resilience, of grief and growth. It honours complexity rather than erasing it. As therapists, educators, and human beings, our task is not to provide easy answers but to hold space for difficult truths, and to guide others through them with humility and care.

Global Perspectives on Decolonising Mental Health: Theoretical Foundations

In examining the impact of colonialism on mental health and the journey of decolonisation, it is impossible to overlook the profound contributions of thinkers from Latin America, Africa, the Middle East, South Asia, and Southeast Asia. These voices illuminate how colonial systems shape not only political and economic realities but also individual and collective psyches (Ndlovu-Gatsheni, 2013; Tuck & Yang, 2012). Their work offers critical frameworks through which to critique, dismantle, and reimagine psychotherapy, grounding it in a more inclusive and culturally attuned praxis (Gone, 2021; Kirmayer et al., 2014).

Paulo Freire's seminal Pedagogy of the Oppressed (1970) reimagines liberation through the lens of conscientização (critical consciousness)—a framework with transformative potential for mental health practice. Freire critiques traditional hierarchies in education, but the same critique applies powerfully to psychotherapy's often Eurocentric models, where therapists assume the role of expert, imposing interpretive frameworks rather than fostering mutual dialogue (Watkins & Shulman, 2008). This colonial dynamic, embedded in the therapeutic process, reinforces oppression by denying clients the agency to author their own healing. In contrast, Freire's vision—resonant with McLeod and Cooper's (2012) pluralistic model—frames therapy as a collaborative, consciousness-raising encounter in which clients name their pain, trace its structural roots, and reclaim their narratives (Moane, 2011). For those committed to decolonised care, this demands a transformation of psychotherapy from private, individual treatment into a dialogical, politicised, and collective space for empowerment.

Similarly, Kenyan writer and academic Ngũgĩ wa Thiong'o (who passed away on 28 May 2025, while I was writing this book), in his landmark work Decolonising the Mind (1986), explores how colonialism weaponised language as a tool of domination and psychological control. Language, for Ngũgĩ, was both a site of trauma and a medium of resistance. The imposition of colonial languages disrupted cultural identity and intergenerational knowledge transmission. In the context of therapy, this insight has profound implications. The dominance of Western psychological discourse often forces clients—particularly those from immigrant and diasporic communities—to describe their experiences in alien terms, stripped of emotional resonance and cultural specificity (Bains, 2005; Duran, 2006). For example, a word like sabr in Arabic or hiya in Swahili may carry layers of meaning that English cannot easily capture. Effective decolonised practice requires more than linguistic translation—it demands epistemic translation, where the client's worldview is honoured as valid, whole, and central. Therapists must embrace linguistic diversity as an ethical and clinical imperative, not a symbolic gesture (Sue & Sue, 2016).

From a Pan-African perspective, Frantz Fanon's work as a psychiatrist and revolutionary offers an unflinching critique of colonialism's psychological violence. His concept of the colonised mind reveals how domination becomes internalised—a theft not only of land but of the self. In Fanon's analysis, colonisation breeds what Bulhan (1985) termed "meta-colonial alienation": the dislocation of identity, community, and spiritual meaning. Western psychotherapy, built on individualistic and biomedical assumptions, is often ill-equipped to address such collective and intergenerational wounds. What Fanon documented in Algeria finds its counterpart in Indigenous African frameworks—particularly Ubuntu-informed therapy—which posit that healing must occur in relationship, not isolation (Mkhize, 2004; Van Breda, 2019). These traditions are not nostalgic remnants; they are active, living systems of knowledge that mend the ruptures created by colonial trauma. They remind us that healing is not an internal event alone—it is relational, communal, and ecological.

Latin American thinkers have also shaped the intellectual architecture of decolonised mental health. Eduardo Galeano's Open Veins of Latin America (1971) renders the continent as a wounded body—scarred by extraction yet pulsing with regenerative vitality. This metaphor extends to the therapeutic space, where clients carry histories of colonisation not only as pain but as potential. Narrative therapy, as pioneered by White and Epston (1990), aligns with Galeano's ethos by encouraging clients to reauthor their stories—transforming their scars from sites of shame to evidence of survival and strength. But Galeano's metaphor of the wounded continent finds its political complement in the work of Afro-Brazilian philosopher Abdias do Nascimento. His philosophy of quilombismo, inspired by the autonomous Black communities that resisted enslavement, insists that true healing is collective (Nascimento, 1980). In this vision, therapy becomes a space not only for personal transformation but for rebuilding communal sanctuaries—what Kirmayer et al. (2014) call "communities of resilience."

Together, these thinkers offer a powerful challenge to conventional Western psychotherapy. They remind us that colonisation was never just an event of the past—it is a living structure that continues to shape our institutions, our knowledge systems, and our healing practices (Maldonado-Torres, 2007; Tuhiwai Smith, 2012). To decolonise psychotherapy, then, is not to add cultural elements to an otherwise Western framework. It is to fundamentally reconsider what healing means, who defines it, and whose wisdom we honour in the process.

Colonial Narratives, Structural Violence, and Indigenous Epistemologies

Edward Said's Orientalism (1978) and Arundhati Roy's critique of neoliberal globalisation (The Cost of Living, 1999) together illuminate both the psychological and structural dimensions of colonial violence. Said's framework unveils how Orientalist narratives construct the colonised as perpetually "other," producing what David (2014) identifies as internalised epistemicide—the internal rejection of ancestral knowledge in favour of Westernised performance. In therapy, this manifests when clients dismiss indigenous cosmologies as "backward," or struggle to articulate themselves in languages that fail to capture their emotional and cultural depth.

Roy's analysis extends this critique to the economic terrain, showing how extractive capitalism enacts ongoing colonisation through forced displacement, land dispossession, and the criminalisation of resistance. Her documentation of Adivasi communities in India, pathologised for grieving their expulsion due to dam construction, exemplifies how colonialism repackages its violence as "development"—and how psychiatry can be complicit in this erasure (Roy, 1999).

Together, these perspectives reorient the therapeutic task. A Dalit client's depression cannot be decontextualised from caste-based violence. A Palestinian's trauma must be understood within the reality of continued occupation (Comas-Díaz, 2020). Where Said guides therapists in identifying internalised oppression, Roy demands they confront its structural underpinnings. The result is a shift from conventional therapy to solidarity-based care—a praxis of radical witnessing, resistance validation, and community-grounded healing. Such care might include facilitating community storytelling, documenting state violence for legal advocacy, or validating grief that has been pathologised by state-sanctioned systems of removal.

Roy's assertion that "the private is public, and the public is private" aptly captures the essence of this decolonial approach. There is no neat division between inner pain and political context. The therapist becomes not only clinician but ally and co-struggler, attuned to how power operates within the therapeutic space and the social order alike.

From Southeast Asia, the writings of Filipino nationalist and revolutionary José Rizal offer a transformative framework for decolonising mental health. His work (El Filibusterismo, 1891; Noli Me Tángere, 1887) reveals how cultural erasure produces psychic rupture and calls for healing rooted in cultural reconnection. Rizal's legacy lives on in Sikolohiyang Pilipino (Filipino Psychology), developed by Virgilio Enriquez (1994), which centres indigenous values such as kapwa (shared identity) and pakikipagkapwa-tao (interpersonal connectedness). These principles reject Western individualism and instead affirm relational being as central to psychological wellbeing.

A compelling example of this is seen in Pe-Pua's (2015) work with Overseas Filipino Workers. Many Overseas Filipino Workers suffer from *kaba*—a culturally inflected form of anxiety associated with dislocation, longing, and diasporic responsibility. Western frameworks often mislabel this as generalised anxiety disorder, erasing its cultural roots. A Rizal-informed intervention would instead:

1. Reframe *hiya* (cultural shame) as a legacy of colonial inferiority—not a personal failing.

2. Integrate *kwentuhan* (community storytelling) as both therapeutic practice and cultural reclamation.

3. Incorporate *orasyon* (spiritual healing practices) as culturally grounded tools for trauma processing and restoration.

Here, therapy becomes an act of *pagbabalik-loob*—a return to self, culture, and collective memory. As Rizal described, it is *liwanag sa dilim*—light emerging from darkness. It is through this lens that suffering is not individualised but seen as part of a historical tapestry of survival, endurance, and resistance.

What unites Said, Roy, Rizal, and the other thinkers in this tradition is their insistence that the personal is inherently political. Mental health cannot be abstracted from caste, race, displacement, language loss, or militarised borders. Decolonisation, then, is not a theoretical gesture. It is a lived commitment to challenge what is assumed to be universal, to honour what has been dismissed, and to reimagine healing on pluralistic, relational terms.

This radically repositions our understanding of trauma. Trauma is not merely an individual disorder to be managed; it is a relational, intergenerational, and structural phenomenon—one shaped by legacies of colonialism and sustained by systems of exclusion and marginalisation (Crenshaw, 1989; Duran, 2006).

Decolonising mental health requires more than critique. It calls for praxis—ongoing, embodied, and culturally located work that centres the voices silenced by imperial knowledge systems. As Freire (1970) reminds us, liberation is never solitary. Healing must be done collectively. It must reconcile colonial fracture without romanticising precolonial idealism, weaving futures that are grounded in dignity and justice.

The thinkers in this section leave us with a challenge and an invitation. As clinicians, scholars, and community members, we must:

1. **Hold duality**—critiquing oppressive systems while cultivating flexible, pluralistic practices.

2. **Centre marginalised epistemologies**—not as "add-ons" to the Western canon, but as equally valid systems of knowing.

3. **Embrace healing as spiral**, not linear. Acknowledging that reconnection, like resistance, is cyclical, layered, and nonlinear.

The next chapter, *Trauma and the Colonised Mind*, traces how these fractures manifest intergenerationally, from silenced languages to displaced bodies, and how reconnection becomes resistance.

References

Bains, J. (2005). Race, culture, and psychotherapy. Routledge.

Bulhan, H. A. (1985). Frantz Fanon and the psychology of oppression. Springer.

Comas-Díaz, L. (2020). Liberation psychology. APA Books.

Crenshaw, K. (1989). Demarginalizing the intersection of race and sex: A Black feminist critique of antidiscrimination doctrine. University of Chicago Legal Forum, 1989(1), 139–167.

David, E. J. R. (2014). Internalized oppression: The psychology of marginalized groups. Springer.

Duran, E. (2006). Healing the soul wound: Counseling with American Indians and other Native peoples. Teachers College Press.

Duran, E., & Duran, B. (1995). Native American postcolonial psychology. State University of New York Press.

Enriquez, V. G. (1994). From colonial to liberation psychology: The Philippine experience. University of the Philippines Press.

Fanon, F. (1963). The wretched of the earth (C. Farrington, Trans.). Grove Press.

Fernando, S. (2010). Mental health, race and culture (3rd ed.). Palgrave Macmillan.

Freire, P. (1970). Pedagogy of the oppressed (M. Ramos, Trans.). Continuum.

Galeano, E. (1971). Open veins of Latin America: Five centuries of the pillage of a continent. Monthly Review Press.

Gone, J. P. (2013). Redressing First Nations historical trauma: Theorizing mechanisms for Indigenous culture as mental health treatment. Transcultural Psychiatry, 50(5), 683–706. https://doi.org/10.1177/1363461513487667

Gone, J. P. (2021). Decolonizing mental health: A radical reimagining of healing in the 21st century. Oxford University Press.

hooks, b. (1994). Teaching to transgress: Education as the practice of freedom. Routledge.

Kirmayer, L. J., Dandeneau, S., Marshall, E., Phillips, M. K., & Williamson, K. J. (2009). Rethinking resilience from Indigenous perspectives. Canadian Journal of Psychiatry, 54(2), 84–91. https://doi.org/10.1177/070674370905400203

Kirmayer, L. J., Gone, J. P., & Moses, J. (2014). Rethinking historical trauma. Transcultural Psychiatry, 51(3), 299–319. https://doi.org/10.1177/1363461514536358

Maldonado-Torres, N. (2007). On the coloniality of being: Contributions to the development of a concept. Cultural Studies, 21(2–3), 240–270. https://doi.org/10.1080/09502380601162548

McLeod, J., & Cooper, M. (2012). The handbook of pluralistic counselling and psychotherapy. SAGE.

Mills, C. (2014). Decolonizing global mental health: The psychiatrization of the majority world. Routledge.

Moane, G. (2011). Gender and colonialism: A psychological analysis of oppression and liberation. Palgrave Macmillan.

Nascimento, A. do. (1980). Quilombismo: An Afro-Brazilian political alternative. Journal of Black Studies, 11(2), 141–178.

Ndlovu-Gatsheni, S. (2013). Empire, global coloniality, and African subjectivity. Berghahn.

Ngũgĩ wa Thiong'o. (1986). Decolonising the mind: The politics of language in African literature. James Currey.

Pe-Pua, R. (2015). Empowering overseas Filipino workers through Filipino psychology: A case study in Hong Kong. Asian Journal of Social Psychology, 18(3), 251–259. https://doi.org/10.1111/ajsp.12102

Pe-Pua, R., & Protacio-Marcelino, E. (2000). Sikolohiyang Pilipino (Filipino psychology): A legacy of Virgilio G. Enriquez. Asian Journal of Social Psychology, 3(1), 49–71. https://doi.org/10.1111/1467-839X.00054

Rizal, J. (1887). Noli me tangere. Berliner Buchdruckerei-Aktiengesellschaft.

Roy, A. (1999). The cost of living. Modern Library.

Said, E. W. (1978). Orientalism. Pantheon Books.

Sue, D. W., & Sue, D. (2016). Counseling the culturally diverse: Theory and practice (7th ed.). Wiley.

Tuck, E., & Yang, K. W. (2012). Decolonization is not a metaphor. Decolonization: Indigeneity, Education & Society, 1(1), 1–40.

Van Breda, A. D. (2019). A critical review of resilience theory and its relevance for social work. Social Work/Maatskaplike Werk, 55(1), 1–18. https://doi.org/10.15270/55-1-715

Watkins, M., & Shulman, H. (2008). Toward psychologies of liberation. Palgrave Macmillan.

White, M., & Epston, D. (1990). Narrative means to therapeutic ends. Norton.

Chapter Two

Trauma and the Colonised Mind

"The oppressor seeks to dominate not only the land and resources of the colonised but also their sense of self, their memory, and their dreams." — Frantz Fanon

Trauma, when it takes root in the human psyche, does not simply dissolve with the passage of time. For communities that have lived through colonisation or continue to experience its aftershocks, trauma becomes more than a personal burden—it becomes a collective inheritance. This trauma lives not only in individual memories but in the shared consciousness of families, communities, and entire cultures. Colonisation was never just about land or resource extraction; it was a systematic attempt to dismantle the foundations of identity; how people see themselves, their histories, their kin, and their relationship to place. It is through this violent reshaping of identity that the trauma of colonisation embeds itself into future generations (Kirmayer et al., 2014; Menakem, 2017).

In clinical practice, I have repeatedly encountered how this inherited wound manifests in subtle yet pervasive ways. Clients may present with anxiety, depression, or chronic disconnection, but beneath these symptoms often lies a deeper story. A story rooted in cultural erasure, systemic marginalisation, and internalised inferiority. To work with such trauma is to engage with what Fanon (1963) described as the psychic rupture of colonisation. Yet, while Chapter 1 focused on unpacking that rupture's philosophical and historical roots, this chapter moves toward application: how we recognise and address the colonised mind in therapeutic space.

Reframing the "Othered" Psyche

Clients from colonised or diasporic communities often speak of feeling "split" between identities, cultures, or expectations. These splits are not pathologies in the traditional sense but are symptoms of structural violence. The orientalist gaze, as Said (1978) theorised, creates a distorted reflection that renders the colonised as irrational, exotic, or inferior. This distortion does not remain on the surface, it is internalised. For the individual sitting across from us in therapy, it can feel like a war between the self they know internally and the one reflected back to them by a society that devalues their being (David et al., 2019).

This internal conflict is frequently misdiagnosed. Therapists unfamiliar with the impact of colonialism may perceive cultural ambivalence as identity confusion, inherited grief as depressive disorder, or spiritual longing as dissociation. It is crucial that we shift our framework. The question is not *"What is wrong with this client?"* but rather *"What historical, cultural, and systemic forces have shaped their suffering?"*

Colonial Trauma as Intergenerational and Embodied

The legacy of colonisation is not confined to a past era, it lives on in the body, the blood, and the neural pathways. The science of intergenerational trauma, as explored in the work of Yehuda and Lehrner (2018), supports what many cultures have long known: trauma is passed down not only through stories and behaviours but through biology. Epigenetic studies show that the stress responses of parents—particularly those who have survived war, genocide, or displacement—can be inherited by their children, affecting their emotional regulation and vulnerability to mental health issues (Gone, 2021).

But trauma is not only inherited through DNA. It is transmitted through language, silence, relational patterns, and even posture. It is present in the way a client flinches at praise, struggles to take up space, or apologises before expressing pain. These inherited behaviours often carry the weight of histories not fully spoken, stories of loss, exile, or survival that have shaped how entire communities relate to safety, belonging, and voice.

The Case of Language Loss and Cultural Disconnection: An Irish Vignette

One client I worked with—a young Irish man in his late twenties—came into therapy not with a dramatic trauma narrative but with what he described as *"a constant ache I can't name."* He struggled with low self-worth and a pervasive sense of not belonging, despite appearing successful and well-adjusted. In exploring his history, it emerged that he had long carried a quiet grief around the Irish language. His grandparents had spoken Gaeilge, but it had not been passed down. As a child, he had been mocked for using Irish words, told that it was "useless" in the modern world. Now, as an adult, he felt the loss deeply but was not sure why.

Initially, he interpreted this sadness as a form of guilt or personal failure. But in the context of therapy, we reframed it as a relational and cultural wound, rooted in Ireland's own colonial history. The British colonial project systematically suppressed the Irish language, outlawing its use in education and governance for centuries. By the mid-20th century, speaking Irish had become associated with backwardness and shame, particularly in working-class and rural areas (Ó hIfearnáin, 2015).

As we unpacked this legacy together, the client's grief transformed. He began to see his feelings not as irrational but as evidence of an unacknowledged ancestral wound. A wound that Ngũgĩ wa Thiong'o (1986) called the "cultural bomb": the destruction of language and heritage as a strategy of domination. Reconnecting with Gaeilge became not only a personal goal but a therapeutic act of resistance. He joined a conversation group, started reading Irish poetry aloud at home, and went to a community workshop on Irish placenames and their meanings. For him, healing was not found in symptom reduction but in cultural restoration.

This case exemplifies how trauma work must be culturally situated and historically aware. Had I taken a more traditional path—interpreting his guilt through a CBT framework or challenging his "negative self-talk"; we might have missed the deeper truth entirely. His pain was not a cognitive distortion; it was a generational echo of erasure.

Embodied Echoes of Colonisation

Colonial trauma does not always present itself in obvious forms. It lives in bodies that flinch before speaking, in voices that shrink when challenged, and in shoulders that tense at the mere possibility of confrontation. I have sat with clients whose bodies tell stories they cannot yet articulate, stories passed down from displaced grandparents, colonised parents, or cultures that were told they must assimilate or disappear.

These embodied expressions of trauma often resist conventional Western diagnostic categories. What is called "hypervigilance" in one clinical manual may, in another context, be a survival strategy handed down through generations. A Syrian mother who startles at loud noises may not meet criteria for PTSD—but her startle response is entirely reasonable given her past in a war zone and her present in an uncertain asylum system. Her nervous system is fluent in danger. The challenge is not to pathologise her body but to help her relearn safety without demanding she forget the wisdom that kept her alive.

Here, it is useful to draw from Indigenous, Afrocentric, and diasporic healing practices that have always treated the body as a site of memory. Land-based rituals, rhythmic movement, prayer, ancestral invocation, and food-based ceremonies all offer routes into embodied healing. The therapist's role in a decolonised frame is not to replace these modalities, but to make space for them, validate them, and learn alongside the client how they function in that person's specific cultural and relational context.

Trauma as Relational and Collective

In Western psychology, trauma is often framed as an intrapsychic rupture, a wound that occurs in the individual psyche due to overwhelming experience. But in many non-Western frameworks, trauma is deeply relational. It disrupts not only the internal world but the client's relationship with others, with land, with ancestors, and with future generations (Watkins, 2019).

One Palestinian client told me, "I can't rest because I haven't yet repaired what was broken in my family during the war." In her view, healing was not about her alone. It was about mending ties with those who suffered before her, honouring their struggle, and making space for her children to live differently. Her healing journey began not with introspection, but with collective reconnection—revisiting her grandmother's recipes, planting native seeds in her garden, and telling her children the stories of their family's resistance.

This is not unique to her culture. Across the Middle East, parts of Africa, Latin America, and Indigenous communities worldwide, trauma is often understood through the lens of interpersonal rupture and communal fragmentation. Restoring harmony between people, land, ancestors, and spirit is the necessary precursor to any personal transformation.

Decolonised therapy, then, must reorient its focus. Instead of asking, "How do I help this individual cope?" we might ask, "What has been broken in this person's relationships, their community, their connection to meaning—and how might it be restored?" This approach draws from liberation psychology (Martín-Baró, 1994), African Ubuntu philosophy—often translated as "I am because we are" or "I am because you are" (Mkhize, 2004)—and Indigenous trauma frameworks (Kirmayer et al., 2014), all of which view healing as an inherently relational, communal, and justice-oriented process.

Intersectionality and the Complexity of Pain

Kimberlé Crenshaw's (1989) concept of intersectionality offers a vital lens through which to understand how colonised trauma operates. For many clients, pain is not just about what happened but about how it intersects with race, class, gender, immigration status, language, and ability (Crenshaw, 2017).

Take the example of a young Black woman in Ireland navigating a mental health system where she is already read as angry, dramatic, or "too much."

When she shares her history of racial bullying or housing insecurity, she may be met with sympathy—but also with subtle disbelief, clinical distance, or suggestions of "distorted thinking." If she refuses a psychiatric label or challenges the system, she may be perceived as "non-compliant." In truth, her resistance may be the healthiest part of her mental health struggle (Gilliam et al., 2016).

In such cases, what appears in Western models as "treatment resistance" may actually be a form of survival intelligence. Her reluctance to open up is shaped by years of having her experience dismissed or punished. Her anger may be her clearest boundary. Her mistrust may be what kept her alive in spaces where vulnerability was dangerous.

To support clients like her, therapists must depathologise resistance and reframe it as a trauma-informed, culturally valid response to systemic harm. This does not mean abandoning clinical structure—but it does mean listening differently, asking deeper questions, and validating the wisdom behind the client's choices.

The Role of Language in Liberation or Erasure

Language is one of the most powerful instruments in both the colonisation and decolonisation of the mind. Ngũgĩ wa Thiong'o (1986) spoke of how colonial rule uses language as a *"cultural bomb"*—separating people from their heritage, self-worth, and worldviews by imposing a foreign tongue. In psychotherapy, we often see the remnants of this. Clients are asked to translate complex, ancestral, or spiritual experiences into English or into DSM-approved categories to receive validation and care (Watters, 2010).

But this translation is not neutral. A woman describing visitations from ancestors may be told she is hallucinating. A child engaging in traditional mourning rituals may be labelled as emotionally dysregulated. In these cases, the therapist's language becomes a colonial tool, reducing culturally grounded expressions of grief or spirituality to symptoms.

Therapists working within a decolonised frame must interrogate:

"Is my language serving the client's healing—or upholding a colonial narrative that defines what is real, valid, or sane?"

This means learning to sit with discomfort, to ask what the client's words mean within *their* context, and to value cultural idioms, silence, metaphor, and embodied storytelling as therapeutic tools.

Rewriting the Narrative: The Power of Cultural Reclamation

One of the most radical acts in therapy is helping clients reclaim their story. Many clients from colonised or marginalised communities have internalised narratives of failure, inferiority, or shame—narratives not theirs, but imposed by systems designed to erase their identities (Tuck & Yang, 2012).

A young Iraqi refugee in Jordan once said to me, "I'm supposed to be broken, right? That's why I'm in this room." His painfully sincere question revealed the societal script he had inherited: that refugeehood meant damage and voicelessness. Our work centred not on "fixing" him, but on documenting his resistance—his skill in translating for his family, navigating hostile bureaucracies, and preserving dignity amid daily dehumanisations. These acts were not mere coping mechanisms; they were everyday revolutions against colonial narratives (Dei, 2017).

This re-authoring process (White & Epston, 1990) transforms clients from passive diagnoses into active meaning-makers, capable of defining themselves beyond colonial scripts.

Reconnecting to the Roots: Cultural Grounding as a Path to Healing

Healing from colonial trauma requires restoring severed roots. For many clients, breakthroughs come not from symptom reduction but from reconnection with others, reconnection to ancestral wisdom, cultural traditions, or silenced languages (Gone, 2013).

Consider a young Arab woman in England who seeks therapy, struggling with feelings of shame and alienation after years of being told her people are "backward" or "uncivilised." A decolonised approach might involve honouring her lived experience rather than pathologising her distress, recognising that her emotions are rooted in systemic oppression rather than personal deficiency. Instead of imposing Western therapeutic models, the therapist could create space for her to reconnect with cultural strengths—her grandmother's storytelling, the deep kinship ties of her community, or the collective lifestyle. By validating her anger as a justified response to discrimination and supporting her participation in more Arabi gatherings if she wishes to, or joining multi-cultural groups where she feels welcome, therapy becomes a means of reclaiming pride in her identity. Healing emerges not from "fixing" her to fit dominant norms, but from restoring her sense of belonging and dignity within her own cultural framework.

This reflects decolonised healing's core truth: psychological suffering often stems from disconnection—from land, culture, community, and purpose. Therapy must become a space to reactivate these ties.

Land as Healer

In many cultures, land is relational:
- *Al-ardh* (Arab): Not just soil, but honour

- Indigenous views: Land as ancestor (Simpson, 2017)

A Kurdish client, disillusioned with talk therapy, found voice during park sessions—naming trees in his mother tongue, recalling the trees' scents from home. His healing required not insight alone, but embodied reconnection to place and memory. These activities, as he reported, had a positive impact on his resilience.

These cases demonstrate the shift from Western "trauma processing" to cultural remembering—weaving severed threads of self, story, and spirit back into living wholeness.

Community as Container: Moving Beyond the Individual

One of the most limiting assumptions of Western psychotherapy is that healing happens primarily within the individual. Clients are seen as self-contained units, expected to improve through insight, self-awareness, and emotional regulation (Hwang, 2021). While these elements matter, they often miss the relational dimension that is central to many non-Western worldviews.

In decolonised practice, we understand that healing is most powerful when held in community. A grieving mother may not find peace through mindfulness alone—but through collective mourning, shared songs, or being seen by other women who understand her pain (Wendt & Gone, 2022). A traumatised adolescent may not open up in a room with one adult therapist—but might speak freely in a youth circle, at a dance class, or while helping cook a family meal.

As therapists, our role is to expand the container. That may mean connecting clients to community resources, inviting family members into sessions, or co-creating healing spaces outside the therapy room. It may mean referring to an imam, a community elder, a traditional healer, or a cultural group—not as an "adjunct" to therapy, but as a central part of the healing team.

This model aligns with the philosophy of "solidarity-based care", which recognises that no single therapist or method holds all the answers. Instead of positioning ourselves as experts, we act as co-weavers of healing networks—networks that respect pluralism, cultural sovereignty, and interdependence.

Spirituality and Decolonised Meaning-Making

Spirituality is often a neglected or pathologised element in traditional therapy spaces. Western psychology has historically framed religious or spiritual experiences as "private beliefs" at best—or as signs of delusion, superstition, or regression at worst (Fernando, 2018). Yet, for many clients, spirituality is the core framework through which trauma, suffering, and healing are made intelligible.

I have worked with clients who experienced ancestral dreams, who felt the presence of deceased loved ones, or who turned to prayer and ritual during crises. In many standard therapeutic settings, these expressions would be questioned, reinterpreted, or dismissed. But in a decolonised space, we ask: *What do these experiences mean to you? What wisdom do they carry? What healing can they offer?*

Integrating spirituality does not mean imposing religious views. It means honouring the metaphysical and symbolic languages through which people make meaning. It means creating space for clients to bring their rituals, their songs, their cosmologies, and their grief into the room without fear of clinical judgement.

This approach aligns with Indigenous mental health models (Duran, 2006), African-centred psychologies (Mkhize, 2004), and Islamic psychotherapy frameworks (Abu-Raiya & Pargament, 2011), all of which place spiritual and communal health at the centre—not the margins—of psychological wellbeing.

From Diagnosis to Decolonial Dialogue

The medicalisation of distress—while sometimes necessary—can also be a form of epistemic violence when applied without cultural awareness. A young child who dissociates in class after surviving war is labelled as inattentive. A refugee mother who mistrusts social workers is considered "uncooperative." A Black teenager who expresses anger at racist teachers is written up as "oppositional." In each case, the diagnostic gaze misses the systemic story.

As therapists committed to decolonised practice, we must learn to name what is unseen:

- This child is adapting to trauma.

- This mother has survived state violence.

- This teenager is resisting erasure.

To support this shift, I often invite clinicians to move from the question: "What's wrong with the client?" to: "What has happened to them? What have they survived? What structures shaped this moment?"

This reframing does not discard clinical skill. It deepens it. It aligns our practice not with the logic of categorisation, but with the ethics of solidarity and context. When we diagnose, we name a pattern. When we decolonise, we uncover the narrative beneath the pattern.

Looking Ahead: Toward Decolonised Psychotherapy

If Chapter One asked us to unlearn the colonial frameworks embedded in psychology, this chapter has invited us to feel their imprint in our clients' bodies, languages, and lives—and to listen differently. Decolonised psychotherapy is not a new method. It is a return—to relationality, community, land, story, and justice. It reminds us that clients are not passive recipients of treatment. They are survivors, narrators, ancestors-in-the-making.

As we move into the next chapter, we will explore the practical foundations of a decolonised therapeutic practice—the tools, principles, and frameworks that can guide us in co-creating healing spaces that honour complexity, courage, and cultural wholeness.

Because decolonisation, like therapy, is not a one-time event. It is a lifelong process of listening, remembering, repairing, and returning.

References

Abu-Raiya, H., & Pargament, K. I. (2011). Empirically based psychology of Islam: Summary and critique of the literature. *Mental Health, Religion & Culture, 14* (2), 93–115.

Crenshaw, K. (1989). Demarginalizing the intersection of race and sex: A Black feminist critique of antidiscrimination doctrine. *University of Chicago Legal Forum, 1989* (1), 139–167.

Crenshaw, K. (2017). *On intersectionality: Essential writings.* The New Press.

David, E. J. R., Schroeder, T. M., & Fernandez, J. (2019). *Internalized oppression: The psychology of marginalized groups.* Springer Publishing.

Dei, G. J. S. (2017). *Reframing blackness and black solidarities through anti-colonial and decolonial prisms.* Springer.

Desmangles, L. G. (2020). *The faces of the gods: Vodou and Roman Catholicism in Haiti.* University of North Carolina Press.

Duran, E. (2006). *Healing the soul wound: Counseling with American Indians and other Native peoples.* Teachers College Press.

Fernando, S. (2014). *Mental health worldwide: Culture, globalization and development.* Palgrave Macmillan.

Fernando, S. (2018). *Institutional racism in psychiatry and clinical psychology: Race matters in mental health.* Palgrave Macmillan.

Gilliam, W. S., Maupin, A. N., Reyes, C. R., Accavitti, M., & Shic, F. (2016). *Do early educators' implicit biases regarding sex and race relate to behavior expectations and recommendations of preschool expulsions and suspensions?* Yale University Child Study Center. https://medicine.yale.edu/childstudy/zigler/publications/Preschool%20Implicit%20Bias_final_347099_5379_v1.pdf

Gone, J. P. (2013). Redressing First Nations historical trauma: Theorizing mechanisms for Indigenous culture as mental health treatment. *Transcultural Psychiatry, 50*(5), 683–706.

Gone, J. P. (2018). "It felt like violence": Indigenous knowledge traditions and therapeutic praxis. *Transcultural Psychiatry, 55*(4–5), 548–562. https://doi.org/10.1177/1363461518792960

Gone, J. P. (2021). Decolonizing mental health services for Indigenous communities: A paradigm shift from treatment to healing. *American Psychologist, 76*(8), 1246–1259.

Hwang, K. K. (2021). *Foundations of Chinese psychology: Confucian social relations.* Springer.

Kimmerer, R. W. (2013). *Braiding sweetgrass: Indigenous wisdom, scientific knowledge, and the teachings of plants.* Milkweed Editions.

Kirmayer, L. J., Gone, J. P., & Moses, J. (2014). Rethinking historical trauma. *Transcultural Psychiatry, 51*(3), 299–319.

Martín-Baró, I. (1994). *Writings for a liberation psychology* (A. Aron & S. Corne, Eds.). Harvard University Press.

Menakem, R. (2017). *My grandmother's hands: Racialized trauma and the pathway to mending our hearts and bodies.* Central Recovery Press.

Mkhize, N. (2004). Psychology: An African perspective. In D. Hook (Ed.), *Critical psychology* (pp. 24–52). University of Cape Town Press.

Ngũgĩ wa Thiong'o. (1986). *Decolonising the mind: The politics of language in African literature.* Heinemann.

Ó hIfearnáin, T. (2015). Sociolinguistic vitality of Manx after language death: Promoting the authentic reproduction of a dormant language. *Journal of Multilingual and Multicultural Development, 36*(4), 371–385.

Said, E. W. (1978). *Orientalism.* Pantheon Books.

Simpson, L. B. (2017). *As we have always done: Indigenous freedom through radical resistance.* University of Minnesota Press.

Tuck, E., & Yang, K. W. (2012). Decolonization is not a metaphor. *Decolonization: Indigeneity, Education & Society, 1*(1), 1–40.

Watkins, M. (2019). *Mutual accompaniment and the creation of the commons.* Yale University Press.

Watters, E. (2010). *Crazy like us: The globalization of the American psyche.* Free Press.

Wendt, D. C., & Gone, J. P. (2022). Community mental health for Native Americans: A decolonial approach to collective healing. *American Psychologist, 77*(4), 614–626.

White, M., & Epston, D. (1990). *Narrative means to therapeutic ends.* Norton.

Chapter Three

Decolonising Psychotherapy: Principles and Practices

"The most effective way to destroy people is to deny and obliterate their own understanding of their history." — George Orwell

Psychotherapy, at its core, is a space for uncovering truths; truths carried in our minds, bodies, and past/histories. For those of us working in regions scarred by colonisation, imperialism, and war, this space takes on a sharper, more urgent significance. The truths we navigate are not just personal but political, shaped by histories of displacement, systemic oppression, and survival in the face of attempts to erase not just individuals, but entire cultures.

This chapter, perhaps the longest in this book, delves into the foundations of decolonised psychotherapy from practical in-the-field experiences. To academic colleagues, I acknowledge the density of these concepts; to non-professional readers, I apologise if the terrain feels arduous at times. My aim is to bridge these worlds—to honour complexity while striving for clarity, because these ideas are too vital to remain confined to academia.

I write as a Palestinian psychotherapist who has lived these truths. My work has taken me to detention centres in Libya, refugee camps in Jordan, working with survivors coming from war-torn villages in Yemen, Syria and Iraq, while carrying the heaviness of my personal trauma and personal package of the colonial legacy growing up and starting my career in Palestine. Time and again, I found that the Western tools I trained with, though valuable, were insufficient. They needed to be not merely adapted but dismantled and reimagined at time to fit the cultural and historical realities of those I worked with.

Decolonised psychotherapy begins with recognising this inadequacy. It acknowledges that mainstream mental health frameworks—born of Western individualism, industrialisation, and imperial domination—cannot fully address wounds rooted in colonial histories, cultural dislocation, and systemic violence. These frameworks, like colonialism itself, often demand assimilation: the client must fit the therapy, never the reverse. To bridge this gap, we need principles that are dynamic, pluralistic, and deeply attuned to the intersections of culture, power, and history.

Foundation 1: Cultural Humility: A Lifelong Practice

One of the core principles of decolonised psychotherapy is cultural humility. A term often diluted by its misuse in mainstream psychology. Unlike "cultural competence" (which implies mastery of static cultural knowledge), cultural humility is a lifelong reckoning with ignorance. It requires therapists to approach each client with curiosity, respect, and the recognition that their expertise will always be provisional.

In Palestine, I worked with a man in his forties, a father of four, who had endured imprisonment and torture. He came to therapy not for relief from his pain— he said he had learned to wear it like a second skin—but because his teenage son had begun asking about their family's history. He wanted to pass on a story that honoured both his suffering and his resistance.

His narrative defied Western therapeutic templates. He spoke of pride in enduring torture without betraying his comrades, but also of the loneliness that estranged him from his family. His resilience was collective; his pain, deeply cultural. Even though my British Supervisor would show empathy and understanding, he would always ask me to stick to what CBT says. Cultural humility meant I could not prescribe what his healing "should" look like. Instead, I had to listen, allowing his story to shape our work. I felt stuck between the anvil and the hammer. At the time (2013), my training had not yet shed its Western assumptions. I recall the dissonance of using CBT worksheets with a man whose trauma was inextricable from political resistance. This is the paradox of decolonisation: it asks us to critique the very tools we rely on.

Cultural humility alone, however, is insufficient. Even shared cultural roots can mask profound differences. This brings us to a second principle:

Foundation 2: Intra-Cultural Humility: The Myth of Shared Experience

Intra-cultural humility, a term I coined through practice, is the active recognition that shared heritage does not guarantee shared lived experience. It demands that therapists interrogate how their own internalised frameworks (often Westernised) distort their understanding of clients from *within* their own cultures.

Example 1: white, middle-class therapist in London, raised in relative material security, works with a white, working-class client who grew up in an overcrowded flat in a neglected neighbourhood. The therapist, despite shared ethnicity, may unconsciously frame the client's anxiety and depression as *individual pathology*—perhaps attributing it to "cognitive distortions" or "low self-esteem" (Beck, 1976)—while overlooking the crushing weight of poverty, the single largest social determinant of mental health globally (World Health Organization [WHO], 2014).

The client's "symptoms" are not merely personal: they are the embodied residue of systemic neglect. Food insecurity, chronic stress from unstable housing, and the humiliation of being made to feel "less than" by institutions (Sweeney et al., 2018). When the therapist suggests mindfulness exercises to "manage stress," the client hears a deafening silence about their eviction notice or the damp mould worsening their child's asthma. The therapist's middle-class assumptions—*that time for self-care exists, that safety is a given*—collide with the client's reality, where survival eclipses introspection.

Key Nuance: The therapist, born into middle-class stability, cannot *know* the visceral fear of choosing between heating and meals, nor the self-loathing internalised from a system that blames the poor for their poverty (Friedli & Stearn, 2015). Intra-cultural humility here demands the therapist:

    1. Acknowledge their ignorance of working-class lived experience.

2. Critically interrogate how neoliberal narratives of "personal responsibility" (Mills, 2018) distort their clinical lens.

3. Shift from pathologising to politicising—e.g., exploring how class oppression shapes the client's self-concept.

Example 2: As a Palestinian therapist, I assumed my own experiences of occupation and displacement granted me innate understanding of Iraqi refugees in Jordan. Yet during one session, a young man interrupted my well-intentioned framing of therapy as a "safe space" with a searing truth: *"Safety is a luxury when you don't know who's your friend and who's your enemy."* echoing hooks' (1990) critique of how dominant groups define safety on their own terms (p. 42).

Though our struggles with colonial violence and collective grief overlayed, the nuances of his Iraqi identity, the particularities of sectarian persecution, and the trauma of fleeing ISIS were not mine to claim. My error was assuming solidarity erased difference. Shared oppression does not equate to shared lived experience (Hooks, 1990).

Tool: To counter this, I adopted privilege inventories, documenting how my relative stability (e.g., professional status, Jordanian passport) created power imbalances even with those from my broader cultural world.

Decolonised Response:
- *Traditional approach*: Interpret his anger as "PTSD symptoms" be understanding and exercise unconditional regard (DSM-5; APA, 2013).

- *Decolonised approach*: Name the political context first— *"Your rage makes sense"* do not pathologise his anger. Rather than imposing Western notions of safety and what pathology is, we co-created strategies rooted in his Iraqi lived experience. When he shared that reciting Quran verses and praying grounded him, we wove these practices into sessions, listening briefly to recordings of his favourite *maqam* recitations, discussing the healing wisdom in specific surahs. We explored how singing Iraqi *mawwawil* (poetic folk songs) allowed him to voice both sorrow and resilience through their melancholic yet soothing melodies. Simple sensory anchors—the scent of cardamom in his morning coffee, cloves in chai—became tools to reframe triggers: *"This smell once took you back to loss; now let it remind you of the hands that prepared it for you."* Safety was not found in removing danger, but in reclaiming these fragments of cultural memory as lifelines. I must admit I was not aware of the decolonised approach and felt out of my depth back then, especially with how Western psychotherapy is very uncomfortable in speaking about spirituality, yet I believed it was only ethical to work with the client's preferences and support his resilience.

The Pluralistic Approach and Intra-Cultural Humility

Mick Cooper and John McLeod's (2011) pluralistic approach to therapy provides a vital framework for intra-cultural humility. Their model emphasises collaborative decision-making between therapist and client, rejecting the notion of universal therapeutic efficacy (McLeod, 2017). This becomes particularly salient when working within shared cultural contexts, where assumptions of homogeneity can obscure nuanced differences in lived experience.

During my work with African migrants in Libyan detention centres, standardised approaches like CBT proved inadequate for addressing the complex interplay of trauma, displacement, and cultural identity. Instead, even though I was not aware that I was using a pluralistic framework, it allowed adaptation to individual needs:

- For some, narrative therapy enabled them to reconstruct their migration journeys as acts of agency rather than victimhood

- Others found healing through embodied cultural practices—when guards permitted, we organised sessions where traditional songs played through loudspeakers sparked collective dancing, momentarily transcending their captivity

This flexibility aligns with what Cooper and McLeod (2011) term "metacommunication"—continuously negotiating therapeutic methods with clients. However, intra-cultural humility demands an additional layer: recognising how even shared backgrounds do not guarantee shared worldviews. A Somali-British therapist, for instance, might unconsciously privilege Western-educated perspectives over a client's rural Somali values (Fernando, 2017).

Foundation 3: Power Dynamics in Therapy

Therapeutic relationships inherently reproduce societal power structures, but decolonised psychotherapy demands that we actively disrupt these dynamics rather than passively replicate them. In Libyan detention centres, my role as a therapist was complicated by the mobility denied to those I worked with. This privilege was not just symbolic; it was a tangible reminder of the hierarchies that defined our interactions. Fanon's (1963) analysis of colonial psychology became palpable when detainees initially perceived me as an extension of the systems oppressing them. Their wariness was not resistance to healing but a survival strategy honed by years of systemic betrayal.

To dismantle this dynamic, I had to relinquish the traditional therapist-as-authority model and instead position myself as a co-learner. For example, I began sessions by acknowledging my privilege openly: *"I know my status as professional lets me walk out of here, while you cannot, and it hurts me to witness your living conditions and stolen freedom. That imbalance is real, and it's something we must navigate together."* This transparency disrupted the unspoken power imbalance, creating space for mutual accountability.

One man's resistance to therapy—his monosyllabic responses, his averted gaze—was initially pathologised in my clinical notes as "non-compliance" (DSM-5; APA, 2013). But when I reframed his silence as strategic survival, a form of what Scott (1990) calls *"weapons of the weak,"* the dynamic shifted. In one session, I said: *"Your silence feels like a boundary, a way to protect yourself. Is that right?"* His nod was the first genuine engagement we had shared. Later, he revealed how detainees subverted oppression:

- **Food refusal as bodily autonomy**: Rejecting meals became an act of reclaiming control over their bodies.

- **Prayer circles as covert resistance meetings**: Gatherings framed as religious devotion doubled as spaces to affirm identity and dignity.

- **Dream-sharing as future orientation**: Narratives of life beyond detention kept hope alive, defying the state's attempt to erase their futures.

Practical Steps to Share Power in Therapy

1. Transparent Positionality:
- *Example*: With a working-class client in London, a middle-class therapist can acknowledge their privileged upbringing and asked, *"How might my background blind me to your struggles?"* This invited them to critique my perspective, redistributing epistemic authority.

2. Collaborative Agenda-Setting:
- *Example*: A survivor of police violence chose to spend sessions analysing systemic racism rather than focusing on "symptom management." It can be helpful to use legal documents and news articles as therapeutic texts, centring the client's expertise as a lived-experience scholar.

3. Language as a Tool of Liberation:
- *Example*: A client from a different cultural background corrected my pronunciation of their name. Instead of defensiveness, I thanked them and asked, *"What does your name mean in your language?"* This small act honoured their cultural knowledge as

equal to clinical "expertise."

4. Rejecting Pathologising Labels:
- *Example*: When a refugee client was diagnosed with "adjustment disorder," we agreed together to work on reframing her distress as *"a rational response to inhuman border policies."*

5. Client-Led Rituals:
- *Example*: Allowing a Yazidi survivor of genocide to begin the sessions by lighting a candle for lost relatives. Follow their lead, sit in silence for a moment until they signal readiness to speak. This ritual affirms their autonomy over time, space, and narrative.

Why This Matters?
Decolonised psychotherapy fails if it merely *acknowledges* power without *dismantling* it. By ceding control—of language, pace, and framework—we transform therapy from an instrument of assimilation into a site of co-resistance. As the Palestinian author Mourid Barghouti writes: *"If you want to dispossess a people, the simplest way is to tell their story and start with, 'secondly.'"* In therapy, we must ensure the client owns the pen.

Table 3.1 Dismantling the Hierarchy: From Traditional to Decolonised Therapy

Traditional Therapy	Decolonised Alternative	Example
Therapist as authority	Co-learner model	"Let's navigate this imbalance together."
Pathologising silence	Framing silence as resistance	"Your silence feels like a boundary. Yes?"
Individual symptom focus	Systemic/political lens	"Your rage makes sense under occupation."
Rigid session structure	Client-led rituals	Lighting candles for lost relatives first.
Neutrality claimed	Explicit political grounding	"Therapy can't be neutral in oppression."

Foundation 4: The Myth of Neutrality: Therapy as Political Ground

Therapy should never claim neutrality when it exists within systems of oppression. When I sit with a Palestinian from Gaza, his body tenses at every distant siren, not because of some innate disorder, but because he has learned that loud noises precede destruction. When a Somali man in a Libyan detention centre eyes my notepad with suspicion, seeing it as an interrogation log rather than a therapeutic tool, his reaction speaks to lived experience with systems that document only to control. I understand this mistrust in my bones. Born under occupation, I knew the acrid taste of tear gas before I ever tasted coffee. When a Palestinian mother in Amman wakes screaming from dreams of her demolished home in Jenin, we are not simply therapist and client going through clinical motions. We are witnesses to the same ongoing story of displacement and resilience.

The colonial legacy permeates every aspect of mental health care. It lives in the diagnostic manuals written by Western minds that pathologise normal reactions to abnormal circumstances. It thrives in the unspoken hierarchies that position the therapist as "expert" over the "patient," replicating the very power dynamics that caused the trauma. It reveals itself when political violence gets rebranded as personal pathology, when the crushing weight of systemic oppression gets reduced to "adjustment disorders" or "maladaptive coping."

This is the truth mainstream psychology often avoids naming: our psychological wounds are not random misfortunes or individual weaknesses. They are direct products of political systems and structures of power. The Palestinian child's nightmares, the Syrian refugee's hypervigilance, the African migrant's dissociation - these are not medical conditions to be cured through therapy alone. They are rational responses to irrational violence, logical reactions to illogical oppression.

Consider how a single mother in Ireland, particularly from a working-class background, navigates a system stacked against her. The political architecture ensures childcare costs consume most of her wages while inflexible work hours ignore parenting realities. If she takes time off to care for a sick child, she risks being labelled unreliable. If she requests flexible hours, she is passed over for promotion. The mental toll of constantly fighting to stay afloat - the anxiety over rent payments, the exhaustion of double shifts, the guilt of never being enough – is not simply personal struggle. It is the inevitable result of political choices that undervalue care work, underfund social housing, and maintain gender pay gaps. Her depression is not a chemical imbalance; it is the logical consequence of living in a society that places mothers in economic precarity by design.

As therapists working with survivors of political violence, we must recognise that we are not just treating symptoms. We are dealing with the psychological aftermath of very real political decisions and systemic failures. The mother's insomnia stems from actual night raids. The detainee's trust issues come from real betrayals by authorities. The refugee's depression grows from tangible losses of home and identity.

This understanding changes everything about how we practice. It means our therapy rooms must become spaces where we name these political roots of pain, where we validate that these wounds were inflicted by design rather than by chance, and where we acknowledge that true healing requires justice as much as it requires coping strategies.

The work begins by dismantling the fiction of apolitical therapy and embracing the uncomfortable truth: when political systems create psychological wounds, therapy must at least acknowledge that it is dealing with the consequences. Anything less is complicity dressed up as care.

A helpful tool when working with people surviving or still living under oppression and war is to acknowledge the political system that caused the suffering and oppression and to acknowledge our privilege as therapists in the therapy room. This can allow for more openness. One of the things that helped me acknowledge my privilege in Libyan detention centres was to say before taking notes: *"I acknowledge that when my visit ends, you will still be here. How should we use that truth?"*.

Foundation 5: The Use of Language: Reclaiming Clients' Words for Wounds

Therapy's greatest violence may be its theft of language, how it takes the poetry of survival and reduces it to sterile clinical terms. I learned this truth from those who refused the textbook definitions:

In Balata refugee camp, a grandmother corrected my notes with a wave of her hand: *"You write 'nightmares'? We call it 'the dreams of return' even our sleep knows we belong in the homes we were kicked out of."* Her words taught me that what psychology calls disordered sleep might instead be yearning and remembering. I could not challenge her over words that bring her resilience.

An Iraqi journalist, a survivor of torture I met in Jordan showed me his scars. *"Your textbook calls this 'body memories',"* he said, tracing the raised lines on his arms. *"But these are not memories. They are receipts. Each one proves who held the knife and who looked away."* His framing transformed what medicine sees as symptoms into evidence of crimes and allowed him to reclaim his narrative.

When clients are uncomfortable with professional language, I begin with inquiries that puncture psychology's pretence of neutrality. For example, I ask:

- *"What did your grandmother call this feeling when she had no therapists to name it for her?"*

- *"If your pain had a name in your mother tongue, what would it be?"*

- *"When the soldiers came, what did your body call this sensation before doctors labelled it 'hypervigilance'?"*

The clients' answers to these questions can be compared and contrasted with professional language as an exercise to create a shared vocabulary between therapist and client.

Foundation 6: Pluralism as a Foundation of Decolonised Psychotherapy

A decolonised psychotherapy practice is inherently pluralistic, rejecting the notion of a singular "correct" therapeutic approach in favour of culturally responsive, client-determined healing pathways (Cooper & McLeod, 2011). This aligns with the American Psychological Association's (2017) multicultural guidelines, which emphasise adapting interventions to clients' cultural contexts. My work with Syrian refugees in Jordan exemplified this principle in action: where Western models like CBT failed to resonate, communal Dabke dances and collective singing—practices rooted in Levantine traditions of asabiyyah (social cohesion; Ibn Khaldun, 1377/2005)—became our primary therapeutic modalities.

Key Principles of Pluralistic Decolonised Practice

1. Client as Cultural Expert

Interventions must honour clients' lived expertise (Cooper & McLeod, 2011). Syrian refugees redefined "treatment goals" by prioritising communal storytelling over individual symptom reduction, demonstrating how healing rituals are embedded in cultural identity (Kirmayer et al., 2014).

2. Rejecting Hierarchies of Knowledge

The DSM-5's (APA, 2013) individualistic frameworks often pathologise collective grief. In contrast, decolonised practice elevates Indigenous epistemologies—such as Ibn Khaldun's asabiyyah—that view wellbeing as inseparable from community (Gone, 2013).

3. Structural Humility

Therapists must acknowledge how power shapes access to care (Crenshaw, 1991). With refugees, this meant replacing clinic-based sessions with circles in community centres, where the act of gathering itself resisted displacement's isolation.

Empirical Support

Research validates pluralistic adaptations:

- Group singing reduces PTSD symptoms in refugees by restoring cultural continuity (Fancourt et al., 2016)

- Collective rituals buffer trauma's neurobiological impacts (Hobfoll et al., 2007)

Implementation Example

Traditional psychotherapy might prescribe journaling for grief. A decolonised pluralistic approach instead:

1. Asks: "How did your ancestors mourn?" (Smith, 2012)

2. Incorporates client-identified practices (e.g., Yemeni zār ceremonies)

3. Measures progress through communal metrics (e.g., "reconnected with 3 relatives")

This approach aligns with the APA's (2021) call to decolonise psychological science by centring marginalised healing traditions while challenging Western-dominated paradigms. It requires validating non-Western epistemologies equally and acknowledging how colonial histories shape mental health systems. In practice, this means examining power dynamics in therapeutic relationships, preserving cultural healing practices ethically, and prioritising community-based methods over individual treatment (Gone, 2021).

These principles manifest through revised diagnostic criteria that avoid pathologising cultural differences, treatment guidelines incorporating diverse healing modalities, and collaborative research with marginalised communities. My work with Syrian refugees in Jordan exemplified this approach - using communal Dabke dancing for cultural preservation, co-designing interventions with community elders to address power imbalances, and measuring outcomes through social connection rather than individual symptom checklists.

As Chapter Eight will explore, pluralistic therapy (Cooper & McLeod, 2011) operationalises these decolonial principles through flexible frameworks that honour multiple healing traditions while addressing therapeutic power dynamics. The refugees' experiences demonstrated that meaningful healing begins when therapy stops imposing external frameworks and truly listens - a core theme I will expand in my dedicated examination of pluralistic approaches. The APA's position marks a crucial institutional shift towards the decolonial values that inform this practice.

Foundation 7: Resistance as Healing: Reclaiming Agency in the Face of Oppression

In decolonised psychotherapy, resistance is reconceptualised as both a survival strategy and an assertion of humanity under oppression. It encompasses not only overt political acts but also the daily preservation of identity, language, and cultural memory in the face of systemic erasure (Fanon, 1963; hooks, 1994).

Resistance is a psychological lifeline as well as a political act, a way of asserting one's humanity when systems seek to erase it. In therapy, this might look like a Palestinian teenager refusing to speak the language of occupation during sessions, or a Somali mother in a Libyan detention centre humming lullabies from her childhood during roll call. These are not acts of defiance to pathologise, but evidence of a spirit that refuses to be broken.

Key Dimensions:

1. **Bodily Resistance:** Refusal to comply with dehumanising systems (e.g., hunger strikes)

2. **Cultural Resistance:** Protecting language, traditions, and intergenerational knowledge

3. **Narrative Resistance:** Reclaiming one's story from colonial frameworks

Clinical Implications:

Therapists need to:

- Distinguish between self-destructive behaviours and health-preserving resistance; while remembering even in medical terms, patients can always refuse treatment, and we are not to force anything on our clients that they do not consent to. In terms of suicide harm and homicide risks, it becomes a matter of confidentiality limits, and these limits would have been explained to the clients in the therapy contract at the start.

- Recognise how seemingly "non-compliant" actions may be acts of agency.

- Validate resistance as evidence of resilience rather than pathology.

I remember a young woman from Ramallah who was imprisoned for protesting. When we met, she did not want to talk about her trauma, not at first. What she needed was for someone to recognise that her "symptoms" were also her strength: the nightmares that kept her alert to danger, the anger that fuelled her organising, the way she still wore her *kuffiyeh* despite causing her to become a target. *"They took everything else,"* she said, *"but they couldn't take my pride."* Therapy became a space to honour that pride, not just "process" the pain. Afterward, we explored together how some of the survival responses that reflected strengths such as the nightmares might not be needed anymore to survive after being released from prison and we could work on it then to reduce it.

This is the heart of decolonised practice: understanding that what looks like "non-compliance" in a clinical file might actually be wisdom. A Syrian journalist labelled "paranoid" for documenting regime crimes was not ill, he was preserving truth in a world that wanted it buried. A refugee boy who rejects therapeutic worksheets is not "resistant", he is protecting the last shred of autonomy he has left.

But resistance is not always loud. Sometimes it is a refugee grandmother teaching her granddaughter old prayers in a language the world tries to forget. Sometimes it is a detained Eritrean man tracing maps of his village in the dust, refusing to let exile erase his home. These quiet acts of preservation are just as vital as protests or hunger strikes.

Of course, therapists must tread carefully. Not every act of defiance is life-affirming, as mentioned earlier some can cause harm to innocent people. Our role is not to romanticise resistance blindly, but to listen deeply, to ask: *"What is this act sustaining in you?"* and *"Who benefits when we call it a disorder?"*

In Chapter Five, I will explore how to walk this line, how to nurture the defiant, life-giving parts of resistance while holding ethical boundaries. Because ultimately, therapy should not teach people to adjust to oppression. It should help them reclaim what oppression tried to steal: their voice, their dignity, their right to say *no*. Chapter five will explore language reclamation as therapeutic intervention, body-based resistance practices and ethical dilemmas in supporting resistance movements.

Foundation 8: Relational Ethics: Healing as Collective Practice

At the heart of decolonised psychotherapy lies relational ethics; the understanding that healing thrives in interconnectedness, not isolation. This principle challenges Western psychology's individualistic bias by centring community wisdom and collective care (Gone, 2013).

This approach demands therapists relinquish their role as sole "experts." During my work in Libya's detention centres and war on Ukraine, I saw this through clients' anger at international inaction exposed my own privileged position as a temporary visitor to their suffering. True relational ethics requires what Crenshaw (1991) calls *intersectional humility*, recognising how our multiple identities (therapist, foreigner, temporary resident) shape therapeutic dynamics.

Furthermore, when a Palestinian refugee in Ireland described feeling like an uprooted tree, we did not pathologise his loneliness, we traced its roots to the severed relationships that had sustained him (Freire, 1970). Our work became about replanting:

1. Cultural Anchors
- Relearning his grandmother's recipes to rebuild a sense of continuity.

- Joining a Palestinian group where mourning songs became bridges between exiles.

2. Land as Co-Therapist
- Planting mint in a pot in his kitchen, the one herb that smelled like his morning tea in Palestine.

- Mapping his walk to work using his town's old landmarks ("*This corner smells like the spice market back home*")

3. Collective Redefinitions
- Redefining "progress" as "the day I carried my friend's baby without flinching from joy"

- Marked milestones by how many minutes he could speak of home before his voice shook (from 30 seconds to 20 minutes over six months)

This aligns with Freire's (1970) vision of liberation, not just personal recovery but the restoration of relational ecosystems. Where traditional therapy might have prescribed mindfulness for his isolation, we honoured that his healing required tangible reconnection to the web of relationships that war had torn (Gone, 2013).

Foundation 9: Land & Identity: Reconnecting to the Earth as Healing

Land is the keeper of memory, language, and ancestral wisdom (Tuck & Yang, 2012). It is the foundation of cultural memory, spiritual belonging, and intergenerational resilience. In decolonised psychotherapy, we recognise that displacement and environmental destruction are not just political issues, but psychological wounds that require culturally-grounded healing approaches (Gone, 2013).

Practical Applications:

1. Soil Therapy

- A Palestinian refugee in Dublin kept a small pouch of soil from her family's razed olive grove. During sessions, we developed grounding exercises where she would hold the soil to physically reconnect to her heritage while staying in the here and now. This pouch of soil served as her safety and comfort item.

2. Guerrilla Gardening

- I met with a Syrian refugee in Cork who turned his balcony into a medicinal herb garden using plants from his homeland (za'atar, sage) to heal his soul as he said. The act of tending became:

- A daily ritual of resistance.

- A sensory bridge to his culture.

- A living symbol of regeneration.

3. Ecological Mapping

- For an Iranian client who could not return home, he said he spends hours watching videos of a Vlogger who walks in the streets, mountains, and markets filming live videos from the town this client grew up in. Hence, we created "memory maps" using:

- Google Earth to virtually visit his village.

- Local parks that mirrored his homeland's landscapes.

- Sound recordings of familiar birdsongs.

These practices align with Indigenous healing frameworks that view land as an active participant in wellness (Tuck & Yang, 2012).

Foundation 10: Therapist Accountability: Confronting Our Positionality

Decolonised psychotherapy demands that therapists engage in continuous, sometimes uncomfortable, self-examination of how their privileges and biases shape clinical practice (Watkins & Shulman, 2008). This goes beyond cultural competence, it requires dismantling the hidden hierarchies in therapeutic relationships.

Concrete Accountability Practices:

1. Privilege Documentation
Before seeing a detainee, I journal:
- My mobility privilege (ability to leave the detention centre)

- Language power (using clinical terms they cannot challenge)

- Institutional authority (they might be afraid the guards could get access to my notes)

2. Transparent Positionality
With clients, I explicitly name power differences: "I want to acknowledge that my training uses Western frameworks that may not fit your experience. Please interrupt me when this happens."
3. Supervision as Decolonisation
Working with my supervisor:
- Review cases through an anti-colonial lens when discussing clients from colonised or post-colonised countries.

- Interrogate when "evidence-based" methods erase clients' local knowledge.

- Develop alternative interventions (e.g., replacing CBT worksheets with traditional storytelling).

4. Clinical Humility

When a Gazan client corrected my interpretation of his nightmares ("it's my body remembering the bombing of our tents after we've been displaced south"), I:

- Amended my notes using his language.

- Acknowledge Palestinian trauma frameworks.

- Shared this learning in supervision.

This ongoing accountability aligns with Fanon's (1963) warning about the colonial shadows in healing professions.

These ten foundations form the bedrock of decolonised psychotherapy, a practice that prioritises cultural humility, dismantles power imbalances, and honours the political and historical contexts of suffering. Even though a few concrete examples were used to apply these foundations, the following section turns to the practical tools and techniques that bring these foundations to life, offering therapists more concrete ways to transform theory into healing praxis. From reclaiming language to co-creating rituals of resistance, these methods invite us to step beyond the confines of traditional therapy and into a space where healing is as dynamic, diverse, and defiant as the people it serves.

Tools and Techniques of Decolonised Psychotherapy

The foundations of decolonised psychotherapy challenge rigid clinical frameworks, but true transformation requires actionable methods. These tools—rooted in cultural wisdom, collective healing, and resistance—bridge theory and practice, ensuring therapy aligns with lived realities rather than imposed paradigms. Below are key techniques, each illustrated with practical examples, to guide therapists in fostering culturally responsive, empowering care.

1. Storytelling: Reclaiming Oral Traditions to Reframe Trauma into Resilience

Storytelling transforms therapy from diagnosis to dialogue, centring clients as narrators of their own lives. This tradition manifests cross-culturally: in Ireland, the *seanchaí* (keeper of oral history) preserves intergenerational memory; in West Africa, the *griot* (or *jeli*) chronicles collective resilience through music and epic poetry (Niane, 1965); across Arab cultures, the *Alhakawati* weaves moral and historical narratives through participatory theatre (Shannon, 2006). Indigenous North American traditions entrust *wampum* keepers with recording history through beaded belts and oral recitation (Hill, 2017), while Māori *pūrākau* (mythic storytelling) embeds ecological wisdom within ancestral accounts (Lee, 2009).

In therapeutic practice, these traditions are revitalised: a Somali refugee might reconstruct trauma through *sheeko* (folktales), where proverbs like *"The river that floods remembers its source"* reframe displacement as continuity (Denborough, 2014). A Métis client could map resilience via *aunty stories*—informal kinship narratives that resist colonial erasure (Iseke, 2013). Such methods reject Western individualism, instead positioning healing as a collective act of narrative reclamation. You do not need to be a storyteller as a therapist, the clients will take that role to tell their stories.

2. Decolonised Mindfulness: Rooting Practices in Cultural/Spiritual Contexts

Standard mindfulness often ignores cultural frameworks. Decolonised adaptations might involve a Palestinian client visualising ancestral olive groves during grounding exercises, or an Indigenous Australian client incorporating *dadirri* (deep listening to land) (Atkinson, 2002). For a Hindu client, mantra repetition with a familial deity could replace breath-focused meditation, aligning practice with spiritual identity.

3. Community-Based Healing: Group Therapy Aligned with Communal Decision-Making

Healing thrives in collective spaces. In Māori culture, *whakawhanaungatanga* (relationship-building) circles allow communities to co-determine healing priorities. For example, a group of displaced Māori youth might use shared *waiata* (songs) to process grief, with elders guiding the pace and structure (Smith, 2012). Similarly, Irish Travellers might gather in *cant* (a traditional tent) for peer-led discussions on systemic discrimination, blending modern therapy with nomadic traditions.

4. Rituals and Ancestral Practices: Integrating Ceremonies

Rituals anchor healing in cultural continuity. Sudanese *Zar* ceremonies—where drumming and dance release embodied trauma—can be adapted into therapy for refugee women (Boddy, 1989). For Māori clients, *karakia* (prayers) might open sessions, invoking ancestral support. A Syrian mother might burn *bakhoor* (incense) during sessions, tying the scent to pre-war memories of home.

5. Language Reclamation: The Therapeutic Power of Mother Tongues

Language is not merely a tool for communication but a vessel of cultural memory, emotional nuance, and ancestral wisdom. Colonialism's linguistic violence, the suppression of Indigenous and marginalised languages, has severed many individuals from the words that once named their joys, sorrows, and lived experiences. In decolonised psychotherapy, language reclamation becomes an act of resistance. For example, a therapist working with a Māori client might encourage the use of *te reo Māori* (the Māori language) to articulate emotions that lack direct English equivalents, such as *aroha* (a deep, unconditional love intertwined with grief). Similarly, a diaspora client may write poetry in their mother tongue to access buried memories of home. This practice aligns with Ngũgĩ wa Thiong'o's (1986) assertion that decolonising the mind begins with reclaiming linguistic sovereignty.

6. Somatic Practices: Healing Trauma Through Embodied Wisdom

The body archives colonial violence in ways that transcend cognitive recall. Somatic therapies, rooted in Indigenous and non-Western traditions, offer pathways to release this embodied trauma. For instance, *Capoeira Angola*—an Afro-Brazilian martial art blending dance, music, and spirituality—has been adapted as movement therapy for descendants of enslaved Africans, helping them reconnect with ancestral resilience (Almeida, 1986). Breathwork, too, can be culturally tailored; a Palestinian client might synchronise their breathing with the rhythms of *Dabke*, transforming hypervigilance into rhythmic grounding. Land-based practices, such as gardening with ancestral crops, further anchor healing in ecological memory, as seen in programmes for Native American youth revitalising traditional farming techniques (Gone, 2013).

7. Collective Activism: Therapy as a Catalyst for Social Change

Decolonised psychotherapy recognises that individual healing is inseparable from systemic justice. Collective activism bridges therapeutic work with community organising, empowering clients to transform personal pain into political agency. A clinical example includes partnering with Indigenous land defenders to design "healing walks" where clients participate in environmental restoration—a practice that simultaneously addresses ecological grief and reaffirms cultural sovereignty (Simpson, 2017). For refugees, contributing to oral history projects that document state violence can reframe trauma testimony as a tool for advocacy, aligning with Freire's (1970) concept of *conscientização* (critical consciousness).

8. Participatory Action Research (PAR): Democratising Knowledge Production

PAR challenges the colonial hierarchy of "expert" and "subject" by positioning communities as co-researchers. In Aotearoa (New Zealand), Māori elders and mental health practitioners have collaborated on PAR projects to integrate *mātauranga Māori* (Indigenous knowledge) into suicide prevention programmes (Smith, 2012). Similarly, Somali refugees in London co-designed a PAR-based intervention using *buraanbur* (poetic oral traditions) to address intergenerational trauma. These projects exemplify Chilisa's (2019) call for research methodologies that "reclaim, rename, and redefine" healing on community terms.

9. Narrative Reauthoring: Rewriting Colonial Scripts

Dominant trauma narratives often reduce colonised peoples to victims, erasing their resistance and resourcefulness. Narrative reauthoring disrupts this by spotlighting acts of survival. A therapist might guide a Vietnamese client to explore how their family's *bánh chưng* (Lunar New Year rice cakes) symbolised covert resistance during wartime scarcity (Phùng, 2020). For African American clients, genealogical research into Freedmen's Bureau records can uncover stories of resilience that counter the trauma of slavery. This technique draws on White and Epston's (1990) narrative therapy while centring cultural specificity.

10. Cultural Genograms: Mapping Heritage as Resistance

Traditional genograms track familial mental health patterns; decolonised genograms map historical trauma *and* cultural continuity. A Puerto Rican family's genogram might highlight how *plena* music preserved West African rhythms despite colonial censorship, or how grandmothers used *curanderismo* (folk healing) to treat ailments pathologised by Western medicine (Tuck & Yang, 2012). For Armenian clients, genograms can trace the survival of *lavash* bread-making across generations as a testament to cultural endurance. These visual tools validate what Tuck and Yang term "theories of survival" (2012, p. 21). Hereby, decolonised genograms maps strengths resilience and resistance instead of mapping what would be preserved as weaknesses and pathology.

While these tools offer transformative potential, their implementation requires vigilance against cultural appropriation and tokenism. The following section examines ethical guardrails—from informed consent to community partnership—that ensure decolonised practice remains accountable to those it seeks to serve.

Ethical Foundations of Decolonised Psychotherapy

Decolonised psychotherapy is a radical reorientation of therapeutic ethics that challenges the colonial roots of mental health care. Traditional ethical frameworks often prioritise individual autonomy and professional detachment, mirroring Western individualism. In contrast, while respecting individual autonomy, decolonised ethics centre relational accountability, cultural humility, and systemic justice. Below are seven core principles that guide ethical practice, ensuring therapists honour the complex interplay of power, culture, and history in the healing process.

1. Informed Consent:

A decolonised approach must never be imposed—even with the best intentions. Just as pluralistic therapy (Cooper & McLeod, 2011) emphasises collaborative goal-setting, therapists must explicitly discuss what decolonised work entails and let clients opt in or out without judgment. Here's how this transforms informed consent:

Key Additions:

1. Explicit Framing

"My approach acknowledges how systems like racism or colonialism may affect your mental health. This means we'll explore societal factors alongside personal ones—but only if you're comfortable. Would you like to hear more before deciding?"

2. No Assumptions

- A Caribbean client may reject "decolonisation" language due to internalised stigma but still want to explore ancestral pride through storytelling.

- A South Asian teen might prefer CBT for exam stress *and* later opt into discussing caste trauma.

3. Ongoing Check-Ins

"Last month we focused on systemic factors. How does that feel now? Want to adjust our focus?"

This aligns with pluralism's core tenet: *"The client is the expert on their own preferences"* (McLeod, 2017).

Ethical Imperative within the informed consent: As Freire (1970) cautioned, even liberatory frameworks become oppressive when applied dogmatically. Decolonised therapy must remain *invitational*, not prescriptive. A space where clients author their own healing narratives, whether they engage with decolonisation explicitly or not.

Example Dialogue:

Therapist: *"Before we begin, I want to share how I work. My approach is influenced by decolonised psychotherapy, which means I pay attention to how larger systems—like colonialism, racism, or cultural oppression—might shape your experiences. For some clients, this lens feels empowering. Others prefer to focus on more immediate personal concerns. Both are completely* *valid. How would you like to proceed? We can explore this together, stick to traditional methods, or mix both—it's entirely up to you."*

Client Response Options:

1. "I'd like to try the decolonised approach—I've always felt my anxiety was tied to my family's displacement."

2. "I'm here for stress management tools right now. Maybe we can revisit the systemic stuff later?"

3. "I'm not sure—can you give me an example of how this would look in our sessions?"

Therapist Follow-Up (for Option 3): *"Of course. For instance, if you mentioned feeling 'not good enough' at work, we might explore whether that's tied to workplace discrimination or cultural stereotypes, rather than assuming it's just low self-esteem. But we'd only go there if it resonates for you."*

2. Cultural Appreciation vs. Appropriation: Honouring Lineages

Decolonised practice demands rigorous attribution of healing traditions. A therapist teaching mindfulness must name its Buddhist origins and confront its corporate commodification (Purser, 2019). Similarly, using Indigenous smudging ceremonies requires collaboration with elders—never extraction. As Tuck and Yang (2012) warn: *"Decolonization is not a metaphor"* for superficial inclusion.

3. Client Agency: Rejecting Therapeutic Imperialism

Clients must freely choose—or refuse—decolonised methods without penalty. A refugee rejecting trauma narratives for resilience-focused work is not "resistant"; they are exercising what hooks (1994) calls *"the right to define reality."* Alternatives like medication or CBT should remain accessible without moral judgment.

4. Transparency on Power: Positionality Statements

Therapists must disclose how their identities (e.g., settler, immigrant, class privilege) shape the dynamic. A white therapist might say:

"As someone who benefits from racial privilege, I'll inevitably miss things. Please correct me."

This mirrors Freire's (1970) *"co-intentional education,"* where power imbalances are named, not neutralised.

5. Boundary Flexibility: Cultural Responsiveness Over Rigidity

"Professional distance" can harm collectivist clients. In Māori *hui* (meetings), therapists may accept shared meals or tears—practices that Western ethics might forbid (Smith, 2012). Conversely, some Muslim clients may prefer gender-matched therapists. Flexibility respects what Comas-Díaz (2020) terms *"cultural soul."*

6. Ethical Advocacy: Beyond the Therapy Room

Therapists actively disrupt systems harming clients, such as:

- Writing affidavits for asylum seekers.

- Partnering with mutual aid networks.

- Adapt Electronic Health Record EHRs that pathologise non-Western coping to be more inclusive and multicultural (Gone, 2021).

- Join groups of activists and protests that advocate to eliminate systemic oppression and suffering.

This aligns with Crenshaw's (1989) intersectional praxis: *"Justice isn't additive; it's embedded."*

7. Continuous Reflexivity: Deliberate Practice for Decolonisation

Decolonised psychotherapy requires *deliberate practice*: the systematic repetition, self-assessment, and refinement of clinical skills (Yalom, 2002). This goes beyond passive reflection, demanding structured engagement with one's biases and therapeutic patterns through:

Structured Self-Interrogation

- *"Whose knowledge systems dominate my interventions?"*

- *"Does my adherence to 'evidence-based' protocols silence cultural wisdom?"*

Anti-Romanticisation Checks

- *"Am I idealising resilience to avoid confronting systemic harm?"*

- *"How does my language (e.g., 'resourceful asylum seeker') perpetuate oppressive narratives?"*

Colonial Unlearning

- *"Where does my training pathologise collective suffering (e.g., labelling grief as 'pathological')?"*

Deliberate Practice Protocols

- **Micro-Skill Drills**: Weekly 15-minute role-plays with peers to practice cultural humility (e.g., responding to a client who rejects DSM labels).

- **Session Audits**: Recording and reviewing 1 session/month to identify epistemic biases (e.g., interrupting clients to impose Western frameworks).

- **Feedback Loops**: Client-informed evaluations (e.g., *"Did my approach honour your cultural definitions of healing?"*).

Liberatory Supervision (Watkins & Shulman, 2008)

Adapting Yalom's (2002) emphasis on *"the here-and-now"*, supervision becomes:

- **Biweekly Praxis Circles**: Case discussions focused on power dynamics (e.g., *"How did my class privilege shape this diagnosis?"*).

- **Outcome Mapping**: Tracking client agency metrics (e.g., frequency of co-created interventions vs. prescribed treatments).

A Call to Ethical Courage

These principles are not static rules but living commitments, ones that demand therapists sit with discomfort, centre marginalised voices, and wield privilege as a tool for dismantling, not maintaining, the status quo. As the next chapter explores, this ethical foundation makes possible the most radical act of all: *therapy that transforms not just minds, but worlds.*

Transition to Potential Gaps to Address

While these ethics provide a framework, decolonised psychotherapy must confront two critical gaps:

Digital Decolonisation

Technology often reproduces colonial hierarchies (e.g., algorithmically biased teletherapy platforms). Ethical practice requires creating virtual spaces that honour diasporic communities—such as encrypted apps for Indigenous language revitalisation or online *diaspora circles* moderated by cultural insiders.

Intergenerational Dialogue

Cultural erasure thrives in generational divides. Therapists can facilitate *bridge sessions* where elders share oral histories and youth reinterpret traditions through contemporary lenses—like Somali grandmothers teaching *buraanbur* poetry to teens navigating racism in schools.

These gaps remind us: decolonisation is iterative. As we address them, new challenges will emerge, each demanding the same ethical rigor modelled above.

Chapter three has laid the foundations of decolonised psychotherapy, presenting ten core principles that recentre healing within cultural, historical, and political contexts. From cultural humility and intra-cultural reflexivity to the dismantling of power dynamics and the reclamation of language, these principles challenge the colonial underpinnings of mainstream mental health frameworks. They invite therapists to move beyond individual pathology, honour collective resilience, and co-create therapeutic spaces where the lived expertise of clients guides the process. The tools and techniques discussed—storytelling, somatic practices, and community-based healing—are not mere interventions but acts of resistance, restoring agency to those marginalised by systemic oppression.

Yet, decolonised psychotherapy cannot stop at theory or individual practice. As the ethical framework underscores, this work demands accountability, interrogating privilege, avoiding appropriation, and advocating for systemic change. The potential gaps identified, such as digital decolonisation and intergenerational dialogue, remind us that decolonisation is iterative, requiring continuous adaptation to new challenges.

This sets the stage for Chapter four that will examine how decolonised psychotherapy intersects with social justice. If Chapter three equipped us with principles and tools, Chapter four will explore their application in dismantling structural inequities—poverty, racism, and economic violence—that shape mental health. Together, these chapters argue that therapy must be both a sanctuary for healing and a catalyst for liberation.

Having established *how* to decolonise practice, we now turn to *why* it matters—the stakes of embedding social justice into the very fabric of psychotherapy. Chapter four confronts the systems that render mental health a privilege, not a right, and explores how therapists can become allies in the fight for equity.

Table 3.2: Key Foundations of Decolonised Psychotherapy

Foundation	Core Principle	Practical Application
Cultural Humility	Lifelong learning; rejection of "expert" authority	Therapists document privilege, defer to clients' cultural knowledge.
Intra-Cultural Humility	Recognising diversity within shared identities	A Palestinian therapist questions assumptions about Iraqi refugees' experiences.
Power Dynamics	Transparency about hierarchies (e.g., mobility, language)	"I acknowledge I can leave this detention centre; you cannot. How does this shape our work?"
Myth of Neutrality	Therapy is inherently political	Validating a Gazan client's hypervigilance as rational under bombardment.
Language Reclamation	Replacing clinical terms with clients' lexicons of survival	"What did your grandmother call this feeling before doctors named it 'anxiety'?"
Pluralism	No single "correct" approach; hybridise Western and Indigenous practices	Syrian refugees use dabke dances for trauma processing.
Resistance as Healing	Reframing "symptoms" as acts of defiance (e.g., hunger strikes, cultural preservation)	A jailed protester's nightmares reinterpreted as survival wisdom.
Relational Ethics	Healing is collective, not individual	Planting mint to reconnect a refugee with ancestral land.
Land & Identity	Land as co-therapist in healing	Soil from a razed olive grove becomes a grounding tool.
Therapist Accountability	Continuous self-interrogation of privilege and bias	Supervision questions: "Whose knowledge am I centring? Whom does my framework exclude?"

References

Adams, G., & Salter, P. S. (2007). Health psychology in African settings: A cultural-psychological analysis. *Journal of Health Psychology, 12*(3), 459-473.

Almeida, B. (1986). *Capoeira: A Brazilian art form*. North Atlantic Books.

American Psychiatric Association. (2013). *Diagnostic and statistical manual of mental disorders* (5th ed.).

American Psychological Association. (2017). *Multicultural guidelines*.

Atkinson, J. (2002). *Trauma trails, recreating song lines: The transgenerational effects of trauma in Indigenous Australia*. Spinifex Press.

Barghouti, M. (2000). *I saw Ramallah*. Random House.

Beck, A. T. (1976). *Cognitive therapy and the emotional disorders*. International Universities Press.

Boddy, J. (1989). *Wombs and alien spirits: Women, men, and the Zar cult in northern Sudan*. University of Wisconsin Press.

Chilisa, B. (2019). *Indigenous research methodologies* (2nd ed.). SAGE.

Comas-Díaz, L. (2020). *Liberation psychology: Theory, method, practice, and social justice*. American Psychological Association.

Cooper, M., & McLeod, J. (2011). *Pluralistic counselling and psychotherapy*. SAGE.

Crenshaw, K. (1989). Demarginalizing the intersection of race and sex. *University of Chicago Legal Forum, 1989*(1), 139-167.

Crenshaw, K. (1991). Mapping the margins: Intersectionality, identity politics, and violence against women of color. *Stanford Law Review, 43*(6), 1241-1299.

Denborough, D. (2014). *Retelling the stories of our lives: Everyday narrative therapy to draw inspiration and transform experience*. W.W. Norton & Company.

Fanon, F. (1963). *The wretched of the earth*. Grove Press.

Fernando, S. (2017). *Institutional racism in psychiatry and clinical psychology*. Palgrave Macmillan.

Freire, P. (1970). *Pedagogy of the oppressed*. Continuum.

Friedli, L., & Stearn, R. (2015). Positive affect as coercive strategy: Conditionality, activation, and the role of psychology in UK government workfare programmes. *Medical Humanities, 41*(1), 40-47.

Gone, J. P. (2013). Redressing First Nations historical trauma: Theorizing mechanisms for Indigenous culture as mental health treatment. *Transcultural Psychiatry, 50*(5), 683-706.

Gone, J. P. (2021). *Decolonizing mental health: Indigenous and global perspectives*. Oxford University Press.

Hill, S. M. (2017). *The clay we are made of: Haudenosaunee land tenure on the Grand River*. University of Manitoba Press.

Hook, J. N., Davis, D. E., Owen, J., Worthington, E. L., & Utsey, S. O. (2013). Cultural humility: Measuring openness to culturally diverse clients. *Journal of Counseling Psychology, 60*(3), 353-366.

hooks, b. (1990). *Yearning: Race, gender, and cultural politics*. South End Press.

hooks, b. (1994). *Teaching to transgress: Education as the practice of freedom*. Routledge.

Ibn Khaldun. (1377/2005). *The Muqaddimah: An introduction to history* (F. Rosenthal, Trans.). Princeton University Press.

Iseke, J. (2013). Indigenous storytelling as research. *International Review of Qualitative Research, 6*(4), 559-577.

Kirmayer, L. J., Gone, J. P., & Moses, J. (2014). Rethinking historical trauma. *Transcultural Psychiatry, 51*(3), 299-319.

Lee, J. (2009). Decolonising Māori narratives: Pūrākau as a method. *MAI Review, 2*(3), 1-12.

McLeod, J. (2017). *Pluralistic therapy: Distinctive features*. Routledge.

Mignolo, W. D. (2011). *The darker side of Western modernity: Global futures, decolonial options*. Duke University Press.

Mills, C. (2018). Dead people don't claim: A psychopolitical autopsy of UK austerity suicides. *Critical Social Policy, 38*(3), 1-22.

Ngũgĩ wa Thiong'o. (1986). *Decolonising the mind: The politics of language in African literature*. James Currey.

Niane, D. T. (1965). *Sundiata: An epic of old Mali* (G. D. Pickett, Trans.). Longman. (Original work published 1960)

Phùng, T. (2020). *Decolonizing Vietnamese memory: Food as counter-archive*. Duke University Press.

Purser, R. (2019). *McMindfulness: How mindfulness became the new capitalist spirituality*. Repeater.

Said, E. W. (1993). *Culture and imperialism*. Knopf.

Scott, J. C. (1990). *Domination and the arts of resistance: Hidden transcripts*. Yale University Press.

Shannon, J. H. (2006). Performing al-hakawati: Storytelling in Damascus. *The Drama Review, 50*(4), 172-183.

Simpson, L. (2017). *As we have always done: Indigenous freedom through radical resistance.* University of Minnesota Press.

Smith, L. T. (2012). *Decolonizing methodologies: Research and Indigenous peoples* (2nd ed.). Zed Books.

Sweeney, A., Filson, B., Kennedy, A., Collinson, L., & Gillard, S. (2018). A paradigm shift: Relationships in trauma-informed mental health services. *Advances in Psychiatric Treatment, 24*(5), 319-333.

Watkins, M., & Shulman, H. (2008). *Toward psychologies of liberation*. Palgrave Macmillan.

White, M., & Epston, D. (1990). *Narrative means to therapeutic ends*. Norton.

Wilson, S. (2008). *Research is ceremony: Indigenous research methods*. Fernwood Publishing.

World Health Organization. (2014). *Social determinants of mental health*.

Yalom, I. D. (2002). *The gift of therapy: An open letter to a new generation of therapists and their patients*. Harper Collins.

Chapter Four

Social Justice and Decolonised Psychotherapy

"*There can be no love without justice. Until we live in a culture that recognizes the legitimacy of all people's need for love, justice, and belonging, we will never move beyond shame to live fully and well.*" — bell hooks, All About Love

Social justice represents the fundamental pursuit of equitable distribution of power, wealth, and resources —a vision of the world in which every individual's inherent dignity is actively honoured (Rawls, 1971). At its core, social justice requires dismantling interconnected systems of oppression including, but not limited to, racism, economic inequality, gender discrimination, ableism, and colonial legacies (Young, 1990). For mental health professionals, this means recognising how these structural forces permeate the therapy room. It necessitates an expanded vision of psychotherapy—one that engages not only with individual distress but with the broader imperative of societal transformation (Prilleltensky, 2003).

Decades of epidemiological research affirm that poverty is one of the most potent social determinants of mental health outcomes (Lund et al., 2018). The World Health Organization (2014) confirms that economic deprivation is strongly correlated with heightened rates of depression, anxiety disorders, and post-traumatic stress disorder across global populations. These associations reflect more than just abstract theory; they represent concrete biological realities. Chronic financial insecurity activates sustained stress responses via the hypothalamic-pituitary-adrenal (HPA) axis, creating neurological and physiological vulnerabilities that manifest as mental distress (Evans & Kim, 2013).

When clients live with housing insecurity (Desmond, 2016), food scarcity (Seligman et al., 2010), or unsafe environments (Clark et al., 2008), their psychological symptoms should be understood as rational responses to irrational conditions. Unfortunately, traditional psychotherapy often fails to contextualise these realities, instead framing them through individualised or pathologising lenses (Tseris, 2019).

Viewed from this perspective, the redistribution of wealth and resources becomes essential dimension of mental healthcare (Patel, 2018). Therapeutic interventions cannot succeed if they ignore the material realities shaping a client's distress. Cognitive restructuring, for example, cannot relieve anxiety rooted in imminent eviction (Watkins, 2019), nor can pharmacotherapy alone resolve depression caused by generational poverty (Hudson, 2005). To practise ethically and effectively, therapists must engage with the structural conditions that contribute to mental suffering, while advocating for reforms that address these root causes (Toporek et al., 2006).

My clinical experience across various cultural and political contexts affirms these conclusions. One example is a single mother in her late thirties, working two minimum-wage jobs yet still struggling to meet her family's basic needs. She presented with symptoms of severe depression, but these symptoms were not the result of internal pathology. Rather, they reflected the toll of sustained economic precarity (Inglis et al., 2023) a cyclical entrapment of poverty on psychological wellbeing. Her sense of failure as a parent was not born of neglect, but of the psychological violence enacted by neoliberal labour policies that make survival without burnout nearly impossible (Harvey, 2005).

In this context, traditional therapeutic tools such as mindfulness practices (Kabat-Zinn, 1990) proved insufficient. Our work had to be integrative and systemic. Alongside psychotherapeutic dialogue, supporting this mother in accessing housing advocacy services and labour rights networks, recognising these as therapeutic interventions in themselves (Smith, 2017). In such cases, therapy is not just about internal healing; it must also facilitate material and structural empowerment.

Decolonised psychotherapy compels us to move beyond the narrow individualism that characterises much of Western psychology (Gone, 2013). The dominant biomedical model often pathologises emotional distress while obscuring its sociopolitical roots (Fernando, 2017). This model must be urgently re-examined. Instead, we must reconceptualise mental health as inseparable from collective wellbeing and systemic justice—not only as a matter of ethical responsibility but as a matter of clinical efficacy (Sue et al., 2019; Martín-Baró, 1994).

Racism, for instance, has profound and well-documented impacts on mental health. Meta-analyses show strong associations between racial discrimination and elevated rates of depression, anxiety, and trauma symptoms (Carter et al., 2019; Sibrava et al., 2019; Paradies et al., 2015). For marginalised groups, these psychological burdens are compounded by economic inequality, producing layers of intersectional oppression (Crenshaw, 1991).

In one case, I worked with a white working-class client from an economically deprived urban area. His presenting concerns included low self-esteem and persistent guilt about not being "strong enough." Through our work, it became evident that these self-perceptions were deeply shaped by class-based stigma and systemic exclusion. His internalisation of blame was not a personal failing but a reflection of what Prilleltensky (2003) calls "oppression internalised"—a psychological burden reinforced by both economic hardship and the culture of meritocracy.

Reshaping the Therapeutic Relationship: Power, Voice, and Resistance

Social justice principles fundamentally reshape therapeutic relationships. Traditional hierarchies often position the therapist as expert and the client as passive recipient—an arrangement Michel Foucault (1965) critiqued as a replication of institutional power structures. In a decolonised framework, such dynamics must be actively dismantled. Therapy must instead become a collaborative partnership, where lived experience is recognised as a form of authoritative knowledge (Freire, 1970). The pluralistic approach uses the term 'therapeutic alliance' for it (McLeod, 2017). I sometimes refer to the therapeutic process as *'participatory'* because of the active role both the client and the therapist play in the therapeutic space.

This becomes particularly crucial when working with oppressed or marginalised populations, for whom therapy can simultaneously represent an opportunity for healing and a potential site of retraumatisation (Bryant-Davis, 2019). In these settings, neutrality becomes complicity. Decolonised psychotherapy therefore calls on practitioners to name systemic injustices within the therapeutic encounter—not as political overreach, but as a prerequisite for safety and trust.

One powerful example emerged in my work with a young Palestinian woman who had been imprisoned after participating in protest actions. Her trauma was not solely rooted in the conditions of her detention, but in the broader experience of political violence and identity erasure. Our work was grounded in recognising her resistance as a source of psychological strength. Instead of viewing her anger, grief, or fear through the lens of pathology, we centred them as expressions of moral clarity and cultural survival—what Fanon (1963) understood as resistance against internalised oppression.

Rather than focusing exclusively on symptom reduction, our sessions sought meaning-making, grounded in the concept of post-traumatic growth through political consciousness (Tedeschi & Calhoun, 2009). This echoes Watkins and Shulman's (2008) work on liberation psychology, which positions therapy as a site of *re-humanisation*—a place to reclaim both dignity and agency after enduring systemic harm.

The Therapist as Advocate: Linking Clinical Practice with Structural Change

Extending psychotherapy into the realm of social justice means challenging the traditional boundaries of the therapy room. Therapists must recognise that structural conditions such as lack of affordable housing, racial discrimination, inaccessible healthcare, and exploitative labour markets are not external to therapy, but integral to it. They are factors that feed and perpetuate distress.

A therapist working in this paradigm must actively engage in systemic advocacy. This can include connecting clients to community resources (housing co-ops, mutual aid funds, legal support), amplifying their voices in institutional settings, or supporting collective movements for justice (Toporek et al., 2006). These acts are not separate from therapy; they are part of a more holistic, justice-oriented practice.

One such example is found in the Trauma Recovery Center (TRC) model in San Francisco, which integrates trauma-informed therapy with wraparound services such as legal aid, housing support, and medical care (Dekker et al., 2024). TRCs have shown remarkable outcomes in reducing PTSD symptoms among clients who face intersecting barriers related to poverty, racism, and violence. Proving that when therapy acknowledges and engages with systemic injustice, it becomes exponentially more effective.

A similarly radical rethinking of care can be seen in the Soteria House project, which originated in California and is described in Terry Lynch's *Beyond Prozac: Healing Mental Distress* (2004). Soteria offered a non-medical, residential alternative to hospitalisation for people experiencing first-episode psychosis. Instead of heavy medication and clinical detachment, the model prioritised community, empathy, and respectful human connection. Staff lived alongside residents, offering support rooted in relationship, not authority. Outcomes were striking: many participants recovered without antipsychotic medication and had better long-term social functioning than those treated in traditional psychiatric hospitals.

Soteria illustrates the profound potential of care environments that reject coercion and reframe madness as meaningful. It shows that when distress is met with safety, respect, and relational depth—rather than fear and control—healing becomes not only possible, but transformative. Like the TRC model, it reaffirms that socially conscious, relationally grounded interventions often outperform institutional norms, especially for those whose suffering is linked to trauma, exclusion, and systemic harm.

As Marmot (2015) argues, policies that reduce social inequality are some of the most powerful levers for improving population-level mental health. In this light, advocating for universal healthcare, living wages, and education access becomes not just political action but clinical necessity. As James Baldwin (1963) so powerfully put it: *"Not everything that is faced can be changed, but nothing can be changed until it is faced."*

The Ethical Imperative of Therapist Reflexivity and Positionality

Building on the foundations outlined in Chapter Three, a justice-aligned therapeutic practice requires ongoing self-reflection regarding the therapist's positionality. This involves critically examining how one's race, class, education, language, citizenship, and professional status confer power—even within well-intentioned clinical interactions.

Therapist privilege can create invisible barriers. A clinician may unconsciously perpetuate harmful norms—such as assuming the value of emotional expression, pushing individualistic coping strategies, or privileging Western ideas of "progress"—which may clash with a client's cultural worldview or survival strategies (Sue et al., 2019). Without deep reflexivity, even the most empathetic therapist can inadvertently replicate oppressive dynamics in the guise of care (DiAngelo, 2018).

To address this, Goodman et al. (2004) propose a framework for training therapists as social justice agents, which includes transparency, cultural humility, and accountability to communities. One useful practice I have created for myself is the use of **"Privilege Audits"**—writing reflections on how my socioeconomic mobility, linguistic fluency, or national status might be affecting the space I co-create with clients. These reflections are then discussed openly in supervision. This 'privilege Audits' tool can be found in the appendices in the end of the book.

Another ethical imperative is to acknowledge limitations within the therapy room itself. For instance, when working with a Syrian refugee navigating asylum bureaucracy, I acknowledge the power imbalance during our sessions by naming it: "I know that at the end of this session, I can resume a relatively secure life. That reality may affect how safe this space feels for you, and I would like us to acknowledge it together."

Such honesty does not undermine the therapeutic alliance—it strengthens it.

Reframing Healing as Collective Liberation

Therapy rooted in social justice must also embrace the idea that healing is not solely personal, it is collective. This framework aligns with Audre Lorde's (1984) insistence that "the master's tools will never dismantle the master's house." To decolonise mental health, we cannot rely on therapeutic approaches that reinforce individualism, self-blame, or neutrality in the face of oppression. We must instead centre dignity, belonging, cultural resilience, and relational healing.

This includes interventions that move beyond the individual and into the collective. Healing circles, narrative therapy grounded in cultural storytelling, and group spaces for shared grief are examples. Community dialogue, ancestral rituals, or culturally rooted movement practices can restore connection and dignity. Liberation psychology helps clients name structural violence and reclaim their agency. In some cases, therapy may also involve advocacy—supporting people to navigate unjust systems or participate in collective action. These practices foster not just coping, but transformation.

Intersectionality is crucial here. As Kimberlé Crenshaw (1989; 1991) powerfully demonstrated, systems of power do not operate independently. Oppressions related to race, class, gender, ableism, and migration status intersect to produce unique experiences of marginalisation. A justice-oriented therapist must work from multidimensional frameworks, ensuring no one is left behind. For example, a disabled, undocumented woman of colour may face forms of exclusion that are invisible within any one-axis approach.

Decolonised and justice-informed therapy requires us to name these layers explicitly and adapt our frameworks accordingly. This includes practical strategies like translating materials into mother tongues, adjusting therapeutic pacing for neurodivergent clients, or validating resistance (such as silence or disengagement) as protective strategies rather than symptoms to be "treated."

These insights demand that we shift our therapeutic gaze. Healing cannot be confined to symptom relief, behavioural regulation, or adaptation to unjust systems. A decolonised, socially just psychotherapy recognises that clients do not bring their distress into the therapy room in isolation. It is entangled with histories of violence, ongoing structural harm, and cultural erasure. To respond ethically and effectively, we must widen the frame. Therapy must be a space that not only listens but acts; a space that holds both pain and protest, both grief and possibility.

Reimagining Mental Health Systems: From Inclusion to Transformation

To truly embed social justice within psychotherapy, we must go beyond merely "including" marginalised identities in pre-existing frameworks. Inclusion, while often well-intentioned, risks reinforcing the very structures that perpetuate inequality if it does not interrogate the foundations themselves. Instead, we must ask: Whose knowledge is centred? Whose ways of healing are legitimised? Whose pain is heard and validated?

Decolonised psychotherapy does not aim to tweak the system from within—it seeks to reimagine the system altogether. This requires centring the wisdoms, traditions, and narratives of communities historically excluded from mainstream mental health discourse. It means understanding land, language, memory, and culture as integral to psychological wellbeing. It insists on shared power, cultural agency, and the co-creation of healing spaces.

This reimagining is not abstract. It has already begun in countless grassroots initiatives, mutual aid networks, indigenous mental health collectives, and culturally grounded peer-support spaces. These models do not separate healing from justice, nor do they treat mental health as detached from housing, education, environment, or labour. Rather, they reflect a truth long known to many communities: there is no health without justice, and no healing without dignity.

Table 4.1 Core Social Justice Principles in Decolonised Psychotherapy Practice

Key Social-Justice Principles	Description	Illustrative Example
Structural Awareness	Recognising poverty, racism, housing and labour conditions as core determinants of mental health	Supporting a client's access to housing advocacy alongside psychotherapy sessions (Smith, 2017)
Collaborative Power	Dismantling therapist-expert/client-passive hierarchies in favour of mutual learning	Opening sessions by acknowledging therapist's mobility privilege when working with detained refugees
Therapist Advocacy	Extending clinical practice into systemic change through partnerships with community organisations	Referring clients to legal aid or local mutual-aid networks as part of their care plan (Toporek et al., 2006)
Reflexivity & Positionality	Ongoing self-examination of the therapist's own social power and biases	Conducting "privilege audits" in supervision to identify how practitioner status might shape the therapeutic space
Collective Liberation	Framing healing as inherently connected to social and political freedom, not only individual symptom relief	Celebrating protest actions and cultural rituals as therapeutic expressions of resilience (Fanon, 1963; Lorde, 1984)

Decolonised psychotherapy invites us to go beyond reform and towards transformation—centring collective wisdom, shared power, and cultural agency in every aspect of care. By naming systemic injustices in the therapy room, partnering with communities on material needs, and honouring clients' own knowledges, we create spaces where healing and justice nourish one another. This work is already unfolding in grassroots networks, peer-led support circles, and Indigenous mental health collectives, proving that there truly is no health without justice, and no healing without dignity.

Yet justice is never claimed from a vacuum. Healing demands resistance—the deliberate, often defiant acts by which individuals and communities reclaim agency from systems designed to erase them. In the next chapter, *The Role of Resistance in Healing*, we turn to these acts: the protests that become protests of the soul, the stories that defy silence, and the quiet rituals that stitch identity back together in exile. Here, therapy becomes a space to heal and to reclaim—language, land, and the right to one's own narrative

References

Baldwin, J. (1962). The fire next time. Dial Press.

Baldwin, J. (1985). The price of the ticket. St. Martin's Press.

Bryant-Davis, T. (2019). The cultural context of trauma recovery: Considering the post traumatic stress disorder practice guideline and intersectionality. American Psychologist, 74(1), 101–116.

Carter, R. T., Mazzula, S. L., Victoria, R., Vazquez, R., Hall, S., Smith, S., Sant-Barket, S., Forsyth, J., Bazelais, K., & Williams, B. (2019). Initial development of the Race-Based Traumatic Stress Symptom Scale: Assessing the emotional impact of racism. Psychological Trauma: Theory, Research, Practice, and Policy, 11(8), 899–906.

Clark, C., Ryan, L., Kawachi, I., Canner, M. J., Berkman, L., & Wright, R. J. (2008). Witnessing community violence in residential neighborhoods: A mental health hazard for urban women. Journal of Urban Health, 85(1), 22–38.

Crenshaw, K. (1989). Demarginalizing the intersection of race and sex: A Black feminist critique of antidiscrimination doctrine. University of Chicago Legal Forum, 1989(1), 139–167.

Crenshaw, K. (1991). Mapping the margins: Intersectionality, identity politics, and violence against women of color. Stanford Law Review, 43(6), 1241–1299.

Desmond, M. (2016). Evicted: Poverty and profit in the American city. Crown Publishers.

DiAngelo, R. (2018). White fragility: Why it's so hard for white people to talk about racism. Beacon Press.

Dekker, A. M., Wang, J., Burton, J., & Taira, B. R. (2024). A scoping review of the Trauma Recovery Center model for underserved victims of violent crime. AIMS Public Health, 11(4), 1247–1269. https://doi.org/10.3934/publichealth.2024064

Evans, G. W., & Kim, P. (2013). Childhood poverty, chronic stress, self-regulation, and coping. Child Development Perspectives, 7(1), 43–48.

Fanon, F. (1963). The wretched of the earth (C. Farrington, Trans.). Grove Press. (Original work published 1961)

Fernando, S. (2017). Institutional racism in psychiatry and clinical psychology: Race matters in mental health. Palgrave Macmillan.

Foucault, M. (1965). Madness and civilization: A history of insanity in the age of reason. Pantheon Books.

Freire, P. (1970). Pedagogy of the oppressed (M. B. Ramos, Trans.). Continuum. (Original work published 1968)

Ginwright, S. (2018). Hope and healing in urban education: How urban activists and teachers are reclaiming matters of the heart. Routledge.

Gone, J. P. (2013). Redressing First Nations historical trauma: Theorizing mechanisms for Indigenous culture as mental health treatment. Transcultural Psychiatry, 50(5), 683–706.

Goodman, L. A., Liang, B., Helms, J. E., Latta, R. E., Sparks, E., & Weintraub, S. R. (2004). Training counseling psychologists as social justice agents: Feminist and multicultural principles in action. The Counseling Psychologist, 32(6), 793–837.

Harvey, D. (2005). A brief history of neoliberalism. Oxford University Press.

hooks, b. (2000). All about love: New visions. William Morrow.

Hudson, C. G. (2005). Socioeconomic status and mental illness: Tests of the social causation and selection hypotheses. American Journal of Orthopsychiatry, 75(1), 3–18.

Inglis, G., Jenkins, P., McHardy, F., Sosu, E., & Wilson, C. (2023). *Poverty stigma, mental health, and well-being: A rapid review and synthesis of quantitative and qualitative research*. Journal of Community & Applied Social Psychology, 33(4), 783–806. https://doi.org/10.1002/casp.2677

Kabat-Zinn, J. (1990). Full catastrophe living: Using the wisdom of your body and mind to face stress, pain, and illness. Delta.

Lorde, A. (1984). Sister outsider: Essays and speeches. Crossing Press.

Lund, C., Brooke-Sumner, C., Baingana, F., Baron, E. C., Breuer, E., Chandra, P., Haushofer, J., Herrman, H., Jordans, M., Kieling, C., Medina-Mora, M. E., Morgan, E., Omigbodun, O., Tol, W., Patel, V., & Saxena, S. (2018). Social determinants of mental disorders and the Sustainable Development Goals: A systematic review of reviews. The Lancet Psychiatry, 5(4), 357–369.

Marmot, M. (2015). The health gap: The challenge of an unequal world. Bloomsbury.

Martín-Baró, I. (1994). Writings for a liberation psychology (A. Aron & S. Corne, Eds.). Harvard University Press.

McLeod, J. (2017). Pluralistic therapy: Distinctive features. Routledge.

Paradies, Y., Ben, J., Denson, N., Elias, A., Priest, N., Pieterse, A., Gupta, A., Kelaher, M., & Gee, G. (2015). Racism as a determinant of health: A systematic review and meta-analysis. PLOS ONE, 10(9), e0138511.

Patel, V. (2018). Where there is no psychiatrist: A mental health care manual (2nd ed.). RCPsych Publications.

Prilleltensky, I. (2003). Understanding, resisting, and overcoming oppression: Toward psychopolitical validity. American Journal of Community Psychology, 31(1–2), 195–201.

Rawls, J. (1971). A theory of justice. Harvard University Press.

Seligman, H. K., Laraia, B. A., & Kushel, M. B. (2010). Food insecurity is associated with chronic disease among low-income NHANES participants. The Journal of Nutrition, 140(2), 304–310.

Sibrava, N. J., Bjornsson, A. S., Pérez Benítez, A. C. I., Moitra, E., Weisberg, R. B., & Keller, M. B. (2019). Posttraumatic stress disorder in African American and Latinx adults: Clinical course and the role of racial and ethnic discrimination. American Psychologist, 74(1), 101–116.

Smith, L. T. (2012). Decolonizing methodologies: Research and Indigenous peoples (2nd ed.). Zed Books.

Stiglitz, J. E. (2012). The price of inequality: How today's divided society endangers our future. W. W. Norton.

Sue, D. W., Sue, D., Neville, H. A., & Smith, L. (2019). Counseling the culturally diverse: Theory and practice (8th ed.). Wiley.

Tedeschi, R. G., & Calhoun, L. G. (2009). TARGET ARTICLE: "Posttraumatic Growth: Conceptual Foundations and Empirical Evidence". *Psychological Inquiry, 15*(1), 1–18. https://doi.org/10.1207/s15327965pli1501_01

Toporek, R. L., Gerstein, L. H., Fouad, N. A., Roysircar, G., & Israel, T. (2006). Handbook for social justice in counseling psychology: Leadership, vision, and action. Sage.

Tseris, E. (2019). *Trauma, Women's Mental Health, and Social Justice: Pitfalls and Possibilities* (1st ed.). Routledge. https://doi.org/10.4324/9781315107820

Watkins, M. (2019). Mutual accompaniment and the creation of the commons. Yale University Press.

Watkins, M., & Shulman, H. (2008). Toward psychologies of liberation. Palgrave Macmillan.

Williams, D. R., & Mohammed, S. A. (2009). Discrimination and racial disparities in health: Evidence and needed research. Journal of Behavioral Medicine, 32(1), 20–47.

World Health Organization. (2014). Social determinants of mental health. WHO Press.

Young, I. M. (1990). Justice and the politics of difference. Princeton University Press.

Chapter Five

The Role of Resistance in Healing

"*Resistance is the secret of joy.*" — Alice Walker

Resistance is a profound act of survival and empowerment. In therapy, it can transform the narrative of trauma from one of victimhood to one of agency and resilience. As we saw in Chapter 4, systemic oppression—from economic deprivation to racial violence—shapes mental health in ways that demand more than individual coping strategies. This chapter builds on that foundation by exploring how resistance, whether subtle or overt, becomes a critical force in psychological healing, especially for those navigating legacies of erasure and dehumanisation. It also emphasises the necessity of distinguishing between empowering forms of resistance and actions that may harm individuals or communities. The therapist's role is not to condone harmful acts but to foster a space where healthy, constructive resistance can be understood and validated as a critical part of healing (Watkins & Shulman, 2008; Bryant-Davis, 2019).

For many clients, resistance manifests as a deliberate assertion of identity and humanity in contexts designed to erase them. The example mentioned in Chapter Three of the young Palestinian woman arrested for participating in protests illustrates this powerfully. She endured long hours of interrogation, isolation, and threats, yet her voice carried immense pride when speaking of her activism. *"I wasn't just there for me,"* she explained. *"I was there for my family, for my people. Even if they tried to break me, they couldn't take that away."* This sense of pride and purpose, born from resistance, became a cornerstone of her healing. Therapy did not aim to erase her trauma but helped her integrate it alongside the strength she drew from her defiance (Fanon, 1963; Martín-Baró, 1994).

Resistance as healing is not limited to contexts of overt political oppression. In various displacement settings across Jordan and Palestine, I encountered clients—particularly from Palestine, Iraq, Syria, and Yemen—whose resistance appeared in quieter but no less meaningful forms. One Syrian man spoke of his refusal to forget his home village, insisting on teaching his children the names of each street and hill he remembered as well as stores and what they would sell in these stores. These acts of remembrance served as a way to preserve cultural memory and resist the psychological erosion of displacement (Gone, 2013; Kirmayer et al., 2009). Validating his resistance meant recognising that holding onto memory was not a failure to move on but a way of safeguarding identity in exile.

Fanon (1963) wrote that resistance is not merely a reaction to oppression but an act of reclaiming humanity. This insight challenges traditional Western therapeutic frameworks, which often pathologise defiance or noncompliance as symptoms to be "managed" (Sue et al., 2007). A decolonised therapeutic approach, by contrast, sees resistance as an essential expression of agency, rooted in cultural, historical, and personal identity. Recognising this dynamic requires cultural and intra-cultural humility and an openness to understanding the broader systems that shape a client's life (Smith, 2012; Prilleltensky, 2003).

Forms of Resistance Across Cultures

The forms that resistance take are as varied as the cultural contexts in which they arise. In Indigenous communities, resistance often looks like reclaiming ancestral lands, knowledge, languages, and traditions eroded by colonialism. In therapy, acknowledging this process involves creating space for clients to connect with their cultural heritage and validating its central role in their healing (Hartmann & Gone, 2016). For example, among Syrian and Iraqi clients I worked with in Jordan, acts such as storytelling, cooking traditional dishes, or reciting poetry functioned as tools of both continuity and survival. Supporting this type of resistance meant helping clients explore how their cultural practices provided strength and coherence in the face of systemic loss (Denborough, 2014).

In African contexts, resistance may take on communal forms, such as collective action or solidarity networks that prioritise mutual aid. In Libya, I worked with African migrants who had been locked up in detention centres and abused while trying to cross the Mediterranean Sea. Despite being subjected to extreme dehumanisation, many found strength in prayer circles, communal singing, and the shared retelling of migration stories. These acts were not only spiritual but political—affirmations of life in spaces designed to break it. In therapy, recognising these forms of resistance required understanding how collective identity functions as both a site of trauma and a resource for resilience (Mohatt et al., 2014).

Resistance can also look different in highly individualistic societies, where the assertion of personal boundaries or refusal to assimilate may serve as acts of defiance. For example, a Palestinian friend living in Europe described how she refused to adopt a "neutral" accent at her university, despite subtle pressures. Her decision to retain her voice—literally and metaphorically—became a powerful symbol of self-definition. Therapy in her situation can support her resistance by validating her refusal to conform and exploring how it helped sustain her sense of integrity (hooks, 1990; Delgado Bernal, 2002).

Distinguishing Resistance from Harmful Acts

A critical component of supporting resistance in therapy is the ability to differentiate between empowering acts of defiance and behaviours that may cause harm. Not all forms of resistance contribute to healing, and therapists have an ethical obligation to guide clients toward constructive expressions of agency (Goodman et al., 2004). For example, resistance may manifest in ways that inadvertently perpetuate harm, such as self-sabotaging behaviours or cycles of retaliation. In these cases, therapy should focus on helping clients explore alternative forms of resistance that align with the clients' values and promote long-term wellbeing (Toporek et al., 2006; Sue et al., 2019).

This distinction is particularly important in multicultural contexts, where the cultural meanings of resistance can vary widely. What may be understood as an act of resilience in one culture could be perceived as a challenge to authority in another. This is especially relevant for individuals and communities living under occupation. According to international law—including the Fourth Geneva Convention and United Nations General Assembly resolutions—people under foreign occupation have a recognised right to resist oppression and assert their self-determination (UNGA, 1974; ICRC, 1949). However, such resistance, particularly when it includes political activism or defiance of imposed authority, may be pathologised or misinterpreted in therapeutic contexts—especially by clinicians unfamiliar with the lived realities of colonisation or military rule (Summerfield, 1999; Fernando, 2017). Therapists must therefore cultivate cultural humility and a nuanced understanding of these differences, ensuring that they support resistance in ways that honour clients' identities and lived experiences without reinforcing harmful patterns (Fisher-Borne et al., 2015).

Therapy as a Space for Resistance

A decolonised approach to therapy not only recognises resistance but actively integrates it into the healing process. Therapy becomes a space where clients can reclaim agency through storytelling, language, cultural practice, and connection. Rather than focusing solely on symptom reduction, the therapeutic goal includes enabling clients to name injustice, honour their histories, and reassert control over their lives (Watkins & Shulman, 2008; White & Epston, 1990).

Narrative therapy, for instance, offers powerful techniques for framing resistance not as defiance but as strength. It enables clients to externalise their problems and reauthor their stories in ways that affirm dignity and coherence (Denborough, 2014). In my work with displaced Syrian clients, many shared stories of home, war, and flight, stories often pathologised as intrusive or dissociative in clinical terms. But when given space and validation, these narratives became tools of meaning-making. One man, who had lost his brothers in the war, described returning to his grandmother's poetry in the aftermath. In therapy, we explored how her verses served as emotional anchors. "When I remember her words," he said, "I remember that I am not just loss—I am from somewhere."

Therapists can also encourage resistance by fostering environments of cultural reclamation. This might include integrating rituals, traditional music, storytelling, or language into therapeutic sessions. In Jordan, where I worked with communities impacted by displacement and poverty, living in refugee camps or crowded residential houses, clients often expressed distress in metaphors tied to nature or ancestry. One woman described her anxiety as "a river with no bank." Rather than reframe this in purely cognitive-behavioural terms, I asked her to speak more about the river—its history, its meaning. This metaphor evolved into a shared symbol in our work, a way of grounding her pain within cultural frameworks rather than outside them. Such metaphoric expression, drawn from cultural language, can offer clients a powerful means to articulate pain while maintaining a sense of identity (Kirmayer et al., 2009; Leeming et al., 2004).

Similarly, among African migrants in Libyan detention centres, I observed how shared prayer, chants, and rhythmic tapping were used to manage overwhelming emotions and reclaim a sense of time and place. These embodied acts were not just coping strategies; they were resistance to fragmentation. I observed it amongst migrants from over fifteen different countries in Africa. A man who had survived two failed sea crossings described these acts as "reminders that we are still humans." Therapy supported these forms of expression by making space for them within sessions. In this context, therapy was not about imposing structure but about witnessing and amplifying survival strategies already in use (Gone, 2013; Mohatt et al., 2014).

The Transformative Power of Resistance

Ultimately, resistance in therapy is not only about healing individual trauma but about reclaiming humanity in the face of systemic dehumanisation. It is an act of defiance against systems that seek to silence, oppress, or erase, and it is deeply tied to collective and cultural identities (Fanon, 1963; Martín-Baró, 1994). For many of the people I have worked with, from Palestine to Libya to Ukraine, healing does not mean forgetting—it means holding pain alongside purpose.

One Palestinian client, a young man from Tulkarem, had been imprisoned multiple times for political activism. In therapy, he shared both his nightmares and his memories of protest with equal intensity. Rather than frame his experiences solely through the lens of trauma, we explored how his sense of identity and resistance remained intertwined. "They broke my body," he said, "but they didn't take my story." Through narrative therapy, his resistance was not undone—it was honoured, named, and integrated into a life that still held meaning.

This is the core of what resistance offers: it restores coherence. For those who have been made to feel powerless, resistance becomes the act that re-establishes personal and political narrative. It is, as Freire (1970) insisted, not only about liberating the oppressed but allowing them to name the world and speak it anew.

Cultural Variations in Resistance

The therapeutic significance of resistance varies across cultures, but its presence is universal. In my work with clients from the Middle East and North Africa, resistance often took the form of storytelling passed down through generations; oral histories that served as both personal and communal anchoring. One Yemeni woman, displaced from her village during the war on Yemen, told her children ancestral tales. "If they forget who we are," she said, "then we are defeated." Her storytelling was more than cultural—it was a form of political continuity and maternal resistance.

Among Ukrainian clients displaced during the 2014–2018 conflict, I witnessed another form of resistance: rituals of domestic order. Clients described continuing to plant herbs, brew tea, and keep traditional icons—even in temporary shelters. These gestures, seemingly mundane, provided rhythm and rootedness. They preserved mental structure in moments of chaos and became small, daily victories over dislocation (Kleinman, 1995; Ginwright, 2016).

Such acts mirror what Tuck and Yang (2012) describe as "refusal"—not just resistance to harm, but a refusal to be defined by it. In the therapy room, validating these everyday rituals and cultural expressions allows clients to reclaim control of their narrative, their space, and their identity.

The Therapist's Role in Honouring Resistance

Therapists have a responsibility to ensure that resistance is not only recognised but supported as a healthy and transformative process. However, this involves navigating complex cultural and ethical dimensions. Without careful reflection, well-intentioned therapists may inadvertently invalidate resistance or attempt to mould it into frameworks that are more comfortable or familiar to them (Goodman et al., 2004; DiAngelo, 2018).

A decolonised therapeutic stance means working alongside resistance, not against it. This requires shifting away from pathologising language—such as "non-compliance" or "defence mechanism"—and toward questions like: *What wisdom does this resistance carry? What is it protecting? What story does it tell?*. In doing so, therapists create space for clients to reflect on their actions with dignity and discernment, not shame.

In practical terms, this may include:

- **Co-exploration:** Inviting clients to reflect on the function and meaning of resistance within their cultural and historical contexts.

- **Narrative honouring:** Using narrative therapy to reframe survival strategies as evidence of resilience and clarity rather than dysfunction (White & Epston, 1990).

- **Embodied affirmation:** Supporting rituals, postures, or creative practices that carry resistance through the body—especially vital for those with trauma histories where language may not fully capture experience (Ogden & Fisher, 2015).

- **Cultural humility:** Practising ongoing reflection about the therapist's own positionality, particularly when power differences exist across race, citizenship, class, or education (Fisher-Borne et al., 2015; Smith, 2012).

These approaches are particularly essential when working with individuals navigating intergenerational and communal trauma. A Syrian woman once described to me the therapeutic space as "the only place where I can be angry and still be seen." Her anger was not a rupture in therapy; it was the heart of our work. Validating her right to rage, mourning, and protest was not political correctness; it was clinical precision.

Resistance as Narrative Healing

One of the most transformative ways therapists can support resistance is by helping clients reclaim their narratives. Narrative therapy enables individuals to externalise problem-saturated identities imposed by systems— "displaced," "illegal," "angry," "non-compliant"—and to construct counter-narratives that honour their lived truths (Denborough, 2014).

For instance, a Sudanese client who had been detained in Libya told me, "They wanted me to believe I was nothing." His healing process involved writing letters to his younger self and to those who had harmed him. Not for vengeance, but to reclaim authorship over his story. "I am here," he wrote, "and I will not end quietly." His act of writing was not simply cathartic; it was a deliberate act of narrative resistance.

Therapy, in this way, becomes more than a clinical relationship. It becomes a relational site of rehumanisation, where stories that have been buried, dismissed, or distorted are retrieved, witnessed, and named.

Conclusion: Resistance as Healing in a Global Context

Resistance, when recognised and honoured, becomes a bridge between trauma and transformation. For those facing the legacies of war, colonisation, racism, and forced migration, resistance is not a luxury. It is often the foundation of survival. It manifests in quiet rituals and bold declarations, in speech and in silence, in refusal and in remembrance. In therapy, acknowledging these acts does not detract from psychological care, it deepens it.

This chapter has shown that resistance is not uniform; it is shaped by culture, history, and power. Therapists must develop the cultural humility and clinical courage to meet resistance not with suspicion but with curiosity and reverence. By doing so, we accompany clients not toward assimilation, but toward autonomy.

The next chapter, *Complex Intersections: Migration, Identity, and Decolonising Psychotherapy*, will examine how identities intersect in therapeutic contexts—focusing particularly on racial bias, the concept of *unchilding*, and the dehumanising effects these processes have on Black, Indigenous, and People of Colour including children.

Below is a table summarising the key forms of resistance discussed in this chapter, alongside their expressions and therapeutic significance.

Table 5.1 Forms of Resistance in Therapy

Form of Resistance	Expression	Therapeutic Significance
Quiet Cultural Resistance	Language use, memory preservation, rituals, prayer	Reinforces cultural continuity and personal agency
Narrative Resistance	Reframing trauma, letter writing, story reclamation	Shifts from victimhood to agency and coherence
Embodied Resistance	Movement, music, sensory grounding, symbolic acts (e.g., carrying soil, photos)	Reconnects body to cultural meaning; stabilises nervous system under threat
Political Resistance	Protest, refusal to conform, activism	Validates injustice and integrates identity with collective struggle
Everyday Defiance	Dress, accent, humour, boundaries	Normalises integrity and defiance in hostile or assimilationist environments
Collective Resistance	Group healing, oral tradition, mutual aid, intergenerational storytelling	Anchors healing in shared identity and collective resilience

References

Alexander, M. J. (2006). Pedagogies of crossing: Meditations on feminism, sexual politics, memory, and the sacred. Duke University Press.

Barghouti, M. (2000). *I saw Ramallah* (A. Soueif, Trans.). Bloomsbury.

Bryant-Davis, T. (2019). The cultural context of trauma recovery: Considering the post_traumatic stress disorder practice guideline and intersectionality. *American Psychologist, 74*(1), 101–116.

Bryant-Davis, T., & Ocampo, C. (2006). Racist incident–based trauma. *The Counseling Psy_chologist, 34*(4), 479–500. https://doi.org/10.1177/0011000006287398

Crenshaw, K. (1991). Mapping the margins: Intersectionality, identity politics, and violence against women of color. *Stanford Law Review, 43*(6), 1241–1299.

Delgado Bernal, D. (2002). Critical race theory, Latino critical theory, and critical raced-gen_dered epistemologies: Recognizing students of color as holders and creators of knowledge. *Quali_tative Inquiry, 8*(1), 105–126. https://doi.org/10.1177/107780040200800107

Denborough, D. (2014). *Retelling the stories of our lives: Everyday narrative therapy to draw inspiration and transform experience*. Norton.

DiAngelo, R. (2018). *White fragility: Why it's so hard for white people to talk about racism.* Beacon Press.

Fanon, F. (1963). *The wretched of the earth* (C. Farrington, Trans.). Grove Press. (Original work published 1961)

Fernando, S. (2017). *Institutional racism in psychiatry and clinical psychology: Race matters in mental health*. Palgrave Macmillan.

Fisher-Borne, M., Cain, J. M., & Martin, S. L. (2015). From mastery to accountability: Cultural humility as an alternative to cultural competence. *Social Work Education, 34*(2), 165–181. https://doi.org/10.1080/02615479.2014.977244

Freire, P. (1970). *Pedagogy of the oppressed* (M. B. Ramos, Trans.). Continuum. (Original work published 1968)

Ginwright, S. (2016). *Hope and healing in urban education: How urban activists and teachers are reclaiming matters of the heart*. Routledge.

Gone, J. P. (2013). Redressing First Nations historical trauma: Theorizing mechanisms for Indigenous culture as mental health treatment. *Transcultural Psychiatry, 50*(5), 683–706.

Goodman, L. A., Liang, B., Helms, J. E., Latta, R. E., Sparks, E., & Weintraub, S. R. (2004). Training counseling psychologists as social justice agents: Feminist and multicultural principles in action. *The Counseling Psychologist, 32*(6), 793–837.

Hartmann, W. E., & Gone, J. P. (2016). Psychological-mindedness and American Indian historical trauma: Interviews with service providers from a Great Plains reservation. *American Journal of Community Psychology, 57*(1–2), 229–242. https://doi.org/10.1002/ajcp.12036

hooks, b. (1990). *Yearning: Race, gender, and cultural politics*. South End Press.

hooks, b. (1994). *Teaching to transgress: Education as the practice of freedom*. Routledge.

ICRC. (1949). *Geneva Convention Relative to the Protection of Civilian Persons in Time of War (Fourth Geneva Convention)*. https://ihl-databases.icrc.org/en/ihl-treaties/gciv-1949

Kirmayer, L. J., Sehdev, M., Whitley, R., Dandeneau, S. F., & Isaac, C. (2009). Community resilience: Models, metaphors and measures. *International Journal of Indigenous Health, 5*(1), 62–117. https://doi.org/10.18357/ijih51201012339

Kleinman, A. (1995). *Writing at the margin: Discourse between anthropology and medicine*. University of California Press.

Leeming, D. A., Madden, K., & Marlan, S. (2004). *Encyclopedia of psychology and religion*. Springer.

Martín-Baró, I. (1994). *Writings for a liberation psychology* (A. Aron & S. Corne, Eds.). Harvard University Press.

Mohatt, N. V., Thompson, A. B., Thai, N. D., & Tebes, J. K. (2014). Historical trauma as public narrative: A conceptual review of how history impacts present-day health. *Social Science & Medicine, 106*, 128–136. https://doi.org/10.1016/j.socscimed.2014.01.043

Ogden, P., & Fisher, J. (2015). *Sensorimotor psychotherapy: Interventions for trauma and attachment*. Norton.

Prilleltensky, I. (2003). Understanding, resisting, and overcoming oppression: Toward psychopolitical validity. *American Journal of Community Psychology, 31*(1–2), 195–201.

Ramphele, M. (1993). *A bed called home: Life in the migrant labour hostels of Cape Town*. David Philip Publishers.

Scott, J. C. (1990). *Domination and the arts of resistance: Hidden transcripts*. Yale University Press.

Smith, L. T. (2012). *Decolonizing methodologies: Research and Indigenous peoples* (2nd ed.). Zed Books.

Sue, D. W., Capodilupo, C. M., Torino, G. C., Bucceri, J. M., Holder, A. M. B., Nadal, K. L., & Esquilin, M. (2007). Racial microaggressions in everyday life: Implications for clinical practice. *American Psychologist, 62*(4), 271–286. https://doi.org/10.1037/0003-066X.62.4.271

Sue, D. W., Sue, D., Neville, H. A., & Smith, L. (2019). *Counseling the culturally diverse: Theory and practice* (8th ed.). Wiley.

Summerfield, D. (1999). A critique of seven assumptions behind psychological trauma programmes in war-affected areas. *Social Science & Medicine, 48*(10), 1449–1462. https://doi.org/10.1016/S0277-9536(98)00450-X

Toporek, R. L., Gerstein, L. H., Fouad, N. A., Roysircar, G., & Israel, T. (2006). *Handbook for social justice in counseling psychology: Leadership, vision, and action.* Sage.

Tuck, E., & Yang, K. W. (2012). Decolonization is not a metaphor. *Decolonization: Indigeneity, Education & Society, 1*(1), 1–40.

United Nations General Assembly. (1974). *Resolution 3314: Definition of Aggression.*

Walker, A. (1992). *Possessing the secret of joy.* Harcourt Brace.

Watkins, M. (2019). *Mutual accompaniment and the creation of the commons.* Yale University Press.

Watkins, M., & Shulman, H. (2008). *Toward psychologies of liberation.* Palgrave Macmillan.

White, M., & Epston, D. (1990). *Narrative means to therapeutic ends.* Norton.

Chapter Six

Complex Intersections

Migration, Identity, and Decolonising Psychotherapy

"If we aren't intersectional, some of us, the most vulnerable, are going to fall through the cracks." – Kimberlé Crenshaw

In a world shaped by colonial legacies, global inequality, and nation-state borders, the lived realities of many people, particularly migrants and racialised individuals, are deeply entangled in systems of oppression that manifest across multiple, intersecting dimensions. For psychotherapists engaging in decolonial practice, it is no longer sufficient to understand identity in singular terms. We must recognise how axes such as race, class, gender, sexuality, migration status, language, religion, and ability interlock to produce unique forms of suffering, resistance, and resilience.

This chapter seeks to explore the psychological consequences of such intersections, with a particular emphasis on migration as a site where colonial history, racial capitalism, and modern-day structural violence collide. While earlier chapters have addressed the legacy of colonialism, the need for structural humility, and the role of resistance in healing, this chapter centres the *complexity of layers*—how identity, politics, and power converge in the lives of those marginalised at the intersections.

Intersectionality is not simply a theoretical framework. It is a lived experience for many clients navigating systems—legal, medical, educational, and therapeutic—that fail to account for the compounded nature of their oppression. As therapists, acknowledging this complexity is a fundamental act of justice and care.

Understanding Intersectionality in Decolonised Psychotherapy

Coined by Kimberlé Crenshaw (1989), the term intersectionality was developed to describe how Black women's experiences of discrimination were not adequately captured by either the feminist movement (which often centred white women) or anti-racist activism (which often centred Black men). Crenshaw argued that these movements failed to account for the *interlocking nature* of oppression—how race and gender intersect to produce a distinct experience.

Since then, intersectionality has grown into a foundational concept for analysing how multiple forms of discrimination—related to race, ethnicity, migration status, disability, religion, and beyond—interact with each other in real-world contexts (Cho, Crenshaw, & McCall, 2013; Collins & Bilge, 2016). In psychotherapy, this means refusing to reduce a client's suffering to a single cause. Instead, we attend to how their experiences are shaped by dynamic and overlapping systems of marginalisation.

Importantly, intersectionality is not about creating a hierarchy of suffering. It is about expanding our capacity to understand the unique positionalities that individuals inhabit, and how those positionalities shape their relationship to trauma, healing, and the therapeutic process (Bowleg, 2012; Hancock, 2007).

The Complex Layers of Migration

Migration is a crucible of intersectionality. It involves geographic displacement, often forced or coerced by war, environmental disaster, or economic desperation. But it also involves psychological displacement; A dislocation of identity, belonging, and recognition. Migrants are frequently rendered hyper-visible as threats or invisible as non-beings, stripped of dignity in public discourse and bureaucratic systems (El-Tayeb, 2011; De Genova, 2010).

In Western Europe, this complexity is particularly sharp. A migrant from Eritrea may be read through racialised assumptions, targeted by border regimes, misdiagnosed in clinical settings, and alienated by language barriers. A Syrian refugee may be welcomed under one political regime and vilified under another, her trauma recognised only when it aligns with Western narratives of suffering (Fiddian-Qasmiyeh, 2016). A Somali Muslim woman may face gendered Islamophobia in France while also navigating the lingering effects of postcolonial displacement.

Yet, these complexities are not confined to Western Europe. Migrants in South Africa often encounter xenophobia from host communities despite shared racial backgrounds, shaped by legacies of apartheid and current neoliberal policies (Landau, 2010; Nyamnjoh, 2006). In the Middle East, stateless nations such as Palestinian or Kurdish refugees live under decades-long occupation, facing discrimination not only from occupying powers but sometimes also within host states (Peteet, 2005; Chatty, 2010).

In Latin America, Indigenous migrants from Guatemala or Honduras often confront racism and anti-Indigenous prejudice as they move into urban centres or across borders into the U.S. (Menjívar, 2006). In Southeast Asia, the Rohingya experience both religious and ethnic persecution, with displacement compounded by their statelessness and the dehumanising conditions of refugee camps in Bangladesh (UNHCR, 2022).

This global view forces us to ask: what happens when a Congolese woman migrates to Morocco, or a Haitian man arrives in Chile, or a Palestinian enters Germany? Each carries intersecting traumas: colonial legacies, cultural erasure, racialisation, class struggle, and, often, spiritual exile. Intersectionality thus becomes a global framework for understanding migration not as an isolated event, but as a continuous negotiation with power across borders.

Therapeutic Implications of Intersectional Migration

When a client presents in therapy after displacement, we must do more than assess symptoms. We must ask: What systems shaped their journey? What silences did they learn to survive? Which parts of themselves did they have to bury to be accepted—or to survive border regimes?

The therapist's role is not to simplify but to hold complexity with humility. This includes making space for language, cultural knowledge, spiritual practice, and storytelling as valid forms of self-expression and healing (Gone, 2013; Kirmayer et al., 2014). It also means acknowledging how diagnostic systems such as the DSM and ICD can obscure or pathologise these very expressions when viewed through a monocultural lens (Fernando, 2010; Watters, 2010).

Intersectionality is not only a conceptual tool—it is an ethical demand. In the therapeutic space, it demands that we reject single-axis thinking, de-centre Western norms, and listen carefully to how clients describe their wounds in their own terms.

Intersectionality, Gender, and Sexuality in Psychotherapy

Gender and sexuality are core components of intersectional identity, shaped not only by personal experience but also by colonial histories and contemporary social norms. A decolonial lens acknowledges that Western constructs of gender and sexuality—particularly the binaries of male/female and heterosexual/homosexual—were exported through colonial violence and used to undermine Indigenous, non-Western, and pre-colonial understandings of identity (Lugones, 2007; Oyěwùmí, 1997). In many cultures, gender diversity and non-heteronormative identities were historically recognised and honoured—whether through the *muxes* of Zapotec Mexico, *two-spirit* people in Indigenous North America, or the *hijra* communities of South Asia. Colonial regimes criminalised these identities, embedding gender and sexual oppression into legal, religious, and educational institutions—a legacy that persists globally.

In therapy, this means that queer and trans clients from diasporic or migrant communities may experience layered marginalisation. A queer Syrian refugee in Germany may face homophobia from both their community and their host society, while also navigating racism and xenophobia. A trans West African asylum seeker might experience displacement not only from homeland and family, but also from medical systems that misgender or pathologise them. Western psychological models have historically been complicit in this marginalisation—evident in the long-standing pathologisation of homosexuality and gender variance (Drescher, 2015). Decolonising psychotherapy thus requires not only affirming LGBTQ+ identities but understanding how colonialism, race, religion, migration, and queerness intersect in deeply complex and culturally specific ways (Ritchie & Barker, 2006). Therapists must move beyond generic "affirmative" practices to create space for culturally grounded, intersectionally informed healing that respects both identity and context.

The Racialisation of Islam and the Psycho-politics of Exclusion and Control

In the Americas, European and global imaginary, Islam is not merely a religion—it is often constructed as a racialised threat. Islamophobia, while ostensibly targeting a belief system, functions in practice as a racialised form of oppression. It does not distinguish between religious observance and cultural identity, nor does it limit itself to theological critique. Instead, it renders Muslim bodies—especially those marked by skin colour, clothing, accent, or geography—as inherently suspect (Sayyid, 2014; Bayoumi, 2008). For therapists working within decolonised frameworks, it is essential to understand Islamophobia not simply as religious bias, but as a structural, embodied, and psychological force.

Since 9/11, the global "War on Terror" has enabled states to deepen surveillance, control, and criminalisation of Muslim populations, especially those who are also migrants or racialised minorities. In this context, Islam becomes coded not just as different, but as dangerous. This racialisation has material consequences: increased policing, detainment, visa restrictions, and violent rhetoric across media and politics. In France, for example, Muslim women wearing the hijab are denied access to public employment and education in the name of *laïcité* (secularism), while far-right parties across Europe campaign on explicitly anti-Muslim platforms (Fernando, 2014; Farris, 2017). The racialisation of Islam is so entrenched that even secular or non-practising individuals of Muslim heritage are subjected to it, based purely on name, ethnicity, or skin colour. It even expands to non-Muslim Arabs. I can easily recall two of my Palestinian friends, a Christian and an atheist, who went to study in the USA, and both told me that they suffered from Islamophobic maltreatment in their colleges.

In psychotherapy, these dynamics often remain unnamed. A Somali Muslim woman in Sweden presenting with symptoms of anxiety may never mention the daily harassment she experiences on public transport. A Pakistani man in the UK may avoid discussing his surveillance fears, assuming the therapist will dismiss them as paranoia. A Moroccan adolescent in France may internalise shame about her Arabic accent or religious identity without ever using the word "racism." Islamophobia is rarely the presenting issue—but it often lies beneath the surface of somatic complaints, relational difficulties, or persistent identity fragmentation.

Therapeutic Implications of Islamophobic Contexts

Therapists working with Muslim clients must learn to recognise how Islamophobia affects not only self-perception, but also how safety, trust, and disclosure function in the therapy room. For many, the therapeutic space is not neutral. It echoes institutions where they have been surveilled, dismissed, or pathologised. The assumption of therapeutic neutrality itself can become a barrier to care—particularly when neutrality entails silence around racism, colonial histories, or political violence (Furqan et al., 2022).

Consider the case of a 15-year-old Muslim boy in Germany who stopped attending therapy after two sessions. His therapist had enthusiastically praised his "integration" and encouraged him to "let go of the past," referring to the boy's stories of witnessing bombings in Syria. In doing so, the therapist erased the meaning of trauma, inadvertently reinforcing a colonial script in which healing is only valid when it conforms to Western norms of progress, forgetting, and assimilation. The client did not return. In his silence, we see the consequence of therapy that refuses to engage with political and racial context: retraumatisation through erasure.

Gendered Islamophobia in Clinical Spaces

Muslim women, particularly those who wear visible religious symbols such as the hijab or abaya, are often subjected to a unique form of gendered Islamophobia. This manifests in both public life and therapeutic settings. They are simultaneously constructed as oppressed victims needing liberation and as dangerous symbols of cultural nonconformity (Mahmood, 2005; Amer & Bagasra, 2013). Within clinical contexts, they may be asked to justify their clothing choices, religious values, or familial practices—often under the guise of "cultural understanding." These microaggressions, while subtle, can severely disrupt the therapeutic alliance.

A decolonised therapeutic response must resist the urge to "save" clients from their own cultures. It requires humility, curiosity, and the willingness to engage in ethical witnessing. Rather than interpret a hijab as a symbol of repression, a therapist might ask: *What does this garment mean to you? How does it connect to your sense of self or your spiritual journey?* Asking these questions opens space for meaning-making on the client's terms—not the therapist's.

Islamophobia and the Failure of Diagnostic Models

Western diagnostic frameworks also struggle to make sense of Muslim clients' distress, often pathologising religious experiences. For instance, spiritual visions, dreams, or somatic responses during prayer may be labelled as psychosis or dissociation, rather than contextualised within cultural or religious understandings of healing. This is particularly dangerous given the growing Islamophobic bias embedded in institutional settings, including law enforcement, schools, and hospitals (Ahmanideen & Iner 2024; Laird et al., 2007).

A truly decolonised psychotherapy must challenge these frameworks. It must ask not, "What is wrong with this person?" but "What has this person endured? What structures shaped their suffering? What cultural resources do they draw upon to survive and heal?"

Unchilding and Racial Bias in Therapeutic Spaces

Unchilding is a term that describes the systematic denial of innocence, vulnerability, and protection to racialised children. Originating in Black radical thought, the concept exposes how children of colour—particularly Black, Indigenous and People of Colour youth—are not granted the societal privileges afforded to white children. Instead, they are hyper-visible, prematurely adultified, criminalised, or erased. Recent research underlines how Black and racialised children are systematically denied the societal privileges of childhood, instead perceived as older, more culpable, or threatening. In healthcare settings, such bias leads to distorted threat assessments, skewed diagnostic practices, and violent disparities in care (Koch & Kozhumam, 2022). Qualitative interviews with Black girls and families further reveal experiences of hyper-sexualisation, adultification, and erasure of innocence (Brissett et al., 2025).

In Western therapeutic spaces, children are often framed as "blank slates" or "becomings," entitled to care, protection, and emotional development. But this framing is not extended equally. A 12-year-old white boy with trauma may be labelled as sensitive or struggling. A 12-year-old Black boy with the same symptoms may be described as aggressive, oppositional, or antisocial (Goff et al., 2014). Their behaviour is criminalised rather than contextualised. Their pain is pathologised, not heard.

Racialised children—particularly those who are migrants, refugees, or visibly Muslim—are disproportionately referred for behavioural assessments, excluded from classrooms, or channelled into punitive interventions rather than therapeutic support. Teachers and clinicians often misinterpret cultural expression, grief, or trauma responses as conduct disorders or personality issues (Gilliam et al., 2016; Elliott et al., 2024). These misdiagnoses are rarely benign. They shape not only the treatment pathways available to children, but their sense of self, safety, and trust in mental health professionals.

Unchilding is not just enacted by legal systems or schools—it can also be reproduced within therapy itself. Therapists, shaped by the same societal discourses as everyone else, may unconsciously project bias into their assessments, interpretations, and interventions. Racialised children are more likely to be subjected to surveillance than understanding, more likely to have their behaviour scrutinised than their suffering acknowledged (Kendi, 2019).

A decolonised therapist must ask: *Who do I automatically read as vulnerable? Who do I instinctively feel needs protection? And who do I perceive, even subtly, as dangerous, non-compliant, or defiant?* These questions are not rhetorical; they are ethical imperatives. The gaze of the therapist is never neutral. It is racialised, classed, gendered, and shaped by colonial residue.

Diagnostic frameworks like the DSM-5 and ICD are often presented as objective tools, yet research shows clear racial bias in their application. Black children in the UK and US, for example, are significantly more likely to be diagnosed with conduct disorders and less likely to be diagnosed with ADHD or anxiety—despite displaying similar symptoms (Lau et al., 2012; Snowden, 2001). This discrepancy is not accidental. It reflects how clinicians often misinterpret distress caused by oppression, attributing it instead to stereotypes or pathology rather than underlying trauma or structural harm (Williams et al., 2023). This dynamic is what is commonly referred to as 'diagnostic overshadowing'—the tendency to overlook the true source of distress because it is obscured by preconceived assumptions about identity or diagnosis.

For Muslim children, the picture is equally troubling. In post-9/11 Western societies, Muslim boys are often pre-emptively associated with extremism, while Muslim girls are constructed as oppressed victims in need of "saving" (Puar, 2007; Amer & Bagasra, 2013). These tropes find their way into case notes, treatment plans, and even therapeutic questions. A child mentioning dreams about war may be asked about radicalisation. A girl expressing pride in wearing the hijab may be met with subtle suspicion about coercion or being 'brainwashed'.

Reclaiming the Child in Therapy

To counter unchilding, therapists must actively rehumanise and recontextualise the child. This begins by recognising the child not only as an individual in distress, but as a carrier of collective stories—migration, faith, racial history, and resistance. A decolonised therapist listens not only to the child's words, but to the systems that speak through their skin colour.

This may mean including cultural practices in the therapy room—storytelling, prayer, dance, family presence. It may also mean advocating outside the therapy room—challenging exclusionary school policies, consulting with community leaders, or offering reflective supervision for colleagues perpetuating harm. Most importantly, it means refusing to accept institutional explanations that frame children as broken, dangerous, or deficient.

As therapists, we must ask: *What does it mean to protect a child whose society sees them as a threat? What does it mean to believe in the innocence of a child who has already been judged?* These are not abstract questions. They are the foundation of an ethical, decolonised practice.

Conclusion: Toward an Ethically Grounded, Decolonised Therapeutic Practice

Throughout this chapter, we have examined how identity cannot be disentangled from systems of power. Migration, race, religion, gender, and class do not operate in isolation; they intersect, collide, and compound in ways that deeply shape a person's psyche, relational world, and access to care. Intersectionality is not a peripheral concept in psychotherapy; it is the very terrain on which much of modern suffering is built.

For migrants in Western Europe and beyond, the therapeutic process unfolds within the long shadows of colonisation, displacement, and exclusion. We have seen how racialised migrants are often misunderstood or pathologised not because of what they bring into therapy, but because of what the mental health system refuses to see: history, context, structure. The complexity of migration is flattened into clinical symptoms. Cultural identity is either exoticised or erased. Spirituality is deemed delusion. Resilience is mistaken for compliance.

Islamophobia further complicates these dynamics, embedding suspicion and surveillance into the very institutions meant to provide care. Muslim clients frequently carry with them not just personal trauma, but the weight of public narratives that cast them as suspect, regressive, or "in need of integration." Therapy, when not explicitly decolonised, can easily become another tool of assimilation—where healing is permitted only if it conforms to white, secular, individualistic norms.

In children, these dynamics manifest in perhaps the most tragic way: the stripping away of innocence through the process of unchilding. Racialised and Muslim children are not seen as needing protection but as posing a threat. Their grief is misread as aggression. Their silence is misread as defiance. Their culture and skin colour are framed as pathologies. The therapeutic space, which should be a site of safety and meaning-making, becomes instead a site of misrecognition and harm.

A decolonised approach to psychotherapy demands that we radically reframe how we see our clients—not as isolated cases or diagnostic puzzles, but as individuals embedded in histories of violence and resistance. It demands that we ask different questions:

- Instead of "What is your presenting problem?" we ask, "What has your life demanded of you to survive?"

- Instead of "How can I treat my client's symptoms?" we ask, "What do my client's symptoms reveal about the world they live in?"

- Instead of "How do you adjust?" we ask, "How do we create space for your truth, your language, your memory?"

This is not about adding more cultural competence workshops or tweaking treatment manuals. It is about disrupting the epistemic assumptions that underlie the entire therapeutic model. It is about recognising that neutrality is not neutral, that silence is not safe, and that the therapeutic alliance must be rooted not only in empathy, but in solidarity.

Decolonised psychotherapy in this context is an ethical orientation. It requires us to step away from the illusion of the expert and step into the uncertainty of co-creation. It asks us to let go of the colonial desire to fix according to our preferences and instead to accompany. It asks us to honour knowledge that is oral, embodied, and spiritual. It asks us to name harm even when doing so is uncomfortable, even when it implicates our institutions, our training, or ourselves.

Ultimately, to practise psychotherapy from a decolonised lens is to practise hope—radical, grounded, collective hope. It is the belief that another world of care is possible. A world where Black children are believed. Where migrants are heard in their own languages. Where intersectionality is the very basis of our clinical imagination.

That world begins in the therapy room. But it does not end there.

References

Ahmanideen, G., & Iner, D. (2024). *The interaction between online and offline Islamophobia and anti-mosque campaigns: The literature review with a case study from an anti-mosque social media page.* Sociology Compass, 18(1), Article e13160. https://doi.org/10.1111/soc4.13160

Amer, M. M., & Bagasra, A. (2013). Psychological research with Muslim Americans in the age of Islamophobia: Trends, challenges, and recommendations. *American Psychologist, 68*(3), 134–144. https://doi.org/10.1037/a0032167

Bayoumi, M. (2008). *How does it feel to be a problem? Being young and Arab in America.* Penguin Press.

Bowleg, L. (2012). The problem with the phrase women and minorities: Intersectionality—an important theoretical framework for public health. *American Journal of Public Health, 102*(7), 1267–1273. https://doi.org/10.2105/AJPH.2012.300750

Brissett, D., Jones, T., Brooks, M., Jones, M., Neal, O., Knight, K., Williams, T., Darien, K., Lee Williams, J., Thomas, D., Foster, C., Ginsburg, K., & Dowshen, N. (2025). Adultification of Young Black Females on Their Health and Well-being: A Qualitative Study. *Pediatrics, 155*(6), e2024069110. https://doi.org/10.1542/peds.2024-069110

Chatty, D. (2010). *Displacement and dispossession in the modern Middle East.* Cambridge University Press.

Cho, S., Crenshaw, K. W., & McCall, L. (2013). Toward a field of intersectionality studies: Theory, applications, and praxis. *Signs, 38*(4), 785–810.

Collins, P. H., & Bilge, S. (2016). *Intersectionality.* Polity Press.

Crenshaw, K. (1989). Demarginalizing the intersection of race and sex. *University of Chicago Legal Forum, 1989*(1), 139–167.

De Genova, N. (2010). The deportation regime: Sovereignty, space, and the freedom of move‐ ment. In N. De Genova & N. Peutz (Eds.), *The Deportation Regime: Sovereignty, Space, and the Freedom of Movement* (pp. 33–65). Duke University Press.

Drescher, J. (2015). Out of DSM: Depathologizing homosexuality. *Behavioral Sciences, 5*(4), 565–575. https://doi.org/10.3390/bs5040565

El-Tayeb, F. (2011). *European others: Queering ethnicity in postnational Europe.* University of Minnesota Press.

Elliott, T. R., Choi, K. R., Elmore, J. G., & Dudovitz, R. (2024). *Racial and ethnic disparities in receipt of pediatric mental health care*. Academic Pediatrics, 24(4). https://doi.org/10.1016/j.acap.2024.01.024

Fanon, F. (1963). *The wretched of the earth* (C. Farrington, Trans.). Grove Press.

Farris, S. R. (2017). *In the name of women's rights: The rise of femonationalism*. Duke University Press.

Fernando, S. (2010). *Mental health, race and culture* (3rd ed.). Palgrave Macmillan.

Fernando, M. L. (2014). *The republic unsettled: Muslim French and the contradictions of secularism*. Duke University Press.

Fiddian-Qasmiyeh, E. (2016) 'Representations of Displacement in the Middle East,' Public Culture, 28(3), doi:10.1215/08992363-3511586.

Furqan, Z., Malick, A., Zaheer, J., & Sukhera, J. (2022). Understanding and addressing Islamophobia through trauma-informed care. *CMAJ : Canadian Medical Association journal = journal de l'Association medicale canadienne, 194*(21), E746–E747. https://doi.org/10.1503/cmaj.211298

Gilliam, W. S., Maupin, A. N., Reyes, C. R., Accavitti, M., & Shic, F. (2016). *Do early educators' implicit biases regarding sex and race relate to behavior expectations and recommendations of preschool expulsions and suspensions?* Yale University Child Study Center.

Goff, P. A., Jackson, M. C., Leone, D., Lewis Di Leone, B. A., Culotta, C. M., & DiTomasso, N. A. (2014). The essence of innocence: Consequences of dehumanizing Black children. *Journal of Personality and Social Psychology, 106*(4), 526–545. https://doi.org/10.1037/a0035663

Gone, J. P. (2013). Redressing First Nations historical trauma: Theorizing mechanisms for Indigenous culture as mental health treatment. *Transcultural Psychiatry, 50*(5), 683–706. https://doi.org/10.1177/1363461513487669

Hancock, A. M. (2007). Intersectionality as a normative and empirical paradigm. *Politics & Gender, 3*(2), 248–254.

Kendi, I. X. (2019). *How to be an antiracist*. One World.

Kirmayer, L. J., Gone, J. P., & Moses, J. (2014). Rethinking historical trauma. *Transcultural Psychiatry, 51*(3), 299–319. https://doi.org/10.1177/1363461514536358

Koch, A., & Kozhumam, A. (2022). Addressing Adultification of Black Pediatric Patients in the Emergency Department: A Framework to Decrease Disparities. *Health promotion practice, 23*(4), 555–559. https://doi.org/10.1177/15248399211049207

Laird, L. D., de Marrais, J., & Barnes, L. L. (2007). Portrayals of Somalis in U.S. media and the complicity of psychotherapeutic approaches: A call for contextualized understanding. *Ethnicity & Health, 12*(5), 479–499.

Landau, L. B. (2010). Loving the alien? Citizenship, law, and the future in South Africa's demonic society. *African Affairs, 109*(435), 213–230.

Lau, M., Lin, H., & Flores, G. (2012). Racial/ethnic disparities in health and health care among U.S. adolescents. *Health services research, 47*(5), 2031–2059. https://doi.org/10.1111/j.1475-677 3.2012.01394.x

Lentin, A. (2008). Europe and the silence about race. *European Journal of Social Theory, 11*(4), 487–503.

Lugones, M. (2007). Heterosexualism and the colonial/modern gender system. *Hypatia, 22*(1), 186–209.

Mahmood, S. (2005). *Politics of piety: The Islamic revival and the feminist subject*. Princeton University Press.

Menjívar, C. (2006). Liminal legality: Salvadoran and Guatemalan immigrants' lives in the United States. *American Journal of Sociology, 111*(4), 999–1037.

Nyamnjoh, F. B. (2006). *Insiders and outsiders: Citizenship and xenophobia in contemporary Southern Africa*. Zed Books.

Peteet, J. (2005). *Landscape of hope and despair: Palestinian refugee camps*. University of Penn sylvania Press.

Puar, J. K. (2007). *Terrorist assemblages: Homonationalism in queer times*. Duke University Press.

Ritchie, A., & Barker, M. (2006). 'There aren't words for what we do or how we feel so we have to make them up': Constructing polyamorous languages in a culture of compulsory monogamy. *Sexualities, 9*(5), 584–601.

Sayyid, S. (2014). A measure of Islamophobia. *Islamophobia Studies Journal, 2*(1), 10–25.

Snowden, L. R. (2001). Barriers to effective mental health services for African Americans. *Mental Health Services Research, 3*(4), 181–187.

Watters, E. (2010). *Crazy like us: The globalization of the American psyche*. Free Press.

Williams, M., Osman, M., & Hyon, C. (2023). Understanding the Psychological Impact of Oppression Using the Trauma Symptoms of Discrimination Scale. *Chronic stress (Thousand Oaks, Calif.), 7*, 24705470221149511. https://doi.org/10.1177/24705470221149511

Chapter Seven

Pluralistic Psychotherapy

Through A Decolonial Lens

"If we are truly committed to helping people, we must be open to the reality that no single therapeutic approach can meet the needs of every client. A pluralistic stance is not just practical, it is ethical." — John McLeod

The pluralistic approach to psychotherapy, developed by Mick Cooper and John McLeod, offers a dynamic, client-centred framework grounded in diversity, integration, and adaptability (Cooper & McLeod, 2011). It recognises that no single therapeutic modality can address the full complexity of human experience and thus encourages therapists to work collaboratively with clients to determine goals and draw on approaches that best suit their emotional, cultural, and social contexts.

This ethos resonates strongly with decolonised psychotherapy, which also rejects one-size-fits-all thinking. However, the two frameworks diverge in emphasis. While pluralism promotes methodological openness and respect for client voice, decolonised psychotherapy takes a more radical stance—it interrogates the colonial legacies embedded within psychology itself and explicitly challenges the systems that marginalise or pathologise non-Western ways of knowing (Fernando, 2017; Smith, 2012).

Both models value cultural responsiveness and client empowerment, but decolonised psychotherapy anchors this work in historical and political analysis. It frames healing as an act of resistance and reclamation, not just adaptation. This chapter explores how pluralistic tools can support decolonised aims while acknowledging their limitations, ultimately advocating for a more ethical, contextually grounded therapeutic practice.

As a note to the reader, there will inevitably be some thematic overlap between this chapter and aspects of Chapter 3, particularly regarding pluralism, cultural integration, and methodological flexibility. It is my hope that this overlap reinforces rather than detracts from the clarity of these concepts, offering depth without unnecessary repetition.

Core Principles

1. Collaboration

Pluralistic therapy emphasises joint decision-making and shared exploration of therapeutic direction (Cooper & Dryden, 2016). This mirrors the decolonised emphasis on dismantling hierarchical models of expertise (Freire, 1970; hooks, 1994). However, decolonised practice pushes this further by recognising that collaboration must also involve engaging with cultural knowledge systems, legacies of violence, and systemic injustice (Watkins & Shulman, 2008; Kirmayer et al., 2014). In this context, collaboration is not only therapeutic—it is political and reparative.

2. Individualisation and Diversity

Pluralism tailors therapy to the unique needs of the individual, aligning with decolonised values of cultural sensitivity and respect for diverse traditions (Moodley & Palmer, 2006). Yet while pluralism treats this flexibility as clinical best practice, decolonised psychotherapy frames it as cultural survival. For example, incorporating Qur'anic recitation or storytelling into therapy with a Syrian client is not merely an adaptation—it is part of a larger process of healing erasure and affirming identity (Gone, 2013).

3. Client Agency and Empowerment

Both approaches prioritise the client's role in shaping therapy, challenging traditional power dynamics (Cooper & Dryden, 2016). Decolonised psychotherapy, however, extends this beyond the individual. It views empowerment through a collective and intergenerational lens—particularly for those impacted by racism, migration, and displacement—highlighting that true agency must address structural violence and historical disempowerment (Prilleltensky, 2003; Martín-Baró, 1994; Bryant-Davis, 2019).

Techniques of the Pluralistic Approach in a Decolonised Context

1. Collaborative Goal Setting

In pluralistic therapy, clients and therapists work together to set meaningful, context-sensitive goals (Cooper & McLeod, 2011). This process resonates strongly within decolonised practice, where therapy is not a neutral act but one entangled in histories of power, identity, and cultural survival (Watkins & Shulman, 2008). For clients navigating intergenerational trauma or migration, goals may include reconnecting with ancestral knowledge, reclaiming language, or building a sense of belonging in a culturally hostile environment. These are not merely therapeutic goals but acts of resistance and identity restoration (Kirmayer et al., 2014; Mohammed, 2022).

2. Feedback-Informed Treatment

Pluralistic therapy often incorporates tools such as the Outcome Rating Scale (ORS) and Session Rating Scale (SRS) to track progress and alliance (Duncan et al., 2003). In a decolonised context, these tools can be expanded or adapted to include culturally relevant indicators of wellbeing—such as spiritual balance, collective connectedness, or a renewed sense of cultural agency (Moodley & Palmer, 2006). Therapists may also draw from community consultation or use collaborative ethnographic methods to inform assessment (Huff et al., 2014; Smith, 2012).

3. Cultural Resources and Practices

A strength of the pluralistic model is its openness to a variety of techniques—including cultural and spiritual resources often excluded from Western models. This overlaps significantly with decolonised therapy, which actively integrates non-Western healing traditions, not as supplements but as central practices (Gone, 2013; Fernando, 2017). These might include oral storytelling, ritual cleansing, drumming, visual arts, or communal meals. For example, clients from Arab, West African, or Indigenous communities may find deep resonance in practices grounded in family, land, and ritual memory (Hartmann & Gone, 2016).

4. Narrative Techniques

Narrative therapy is a core method in pluralistic work. Clients are invited to re-author their stories, externalise problems, and name their strengths (White & Epston, 1990). In decolonised practice, this re-authoring takes on a distinctly political tone: it allows clients to reject internalised colonial narratives and reclaim counter-stories rooted in survival, struggle, and joy (Thomas et al., 2018; Delgado Bernal, 2002). For instance, a Libyan migrant may reframe their journey not as a "refugee trauma" but as a legacy of resistance to border violence and displacement.

5. Task Design and Homework

Task-based work in pluralistic therapy—such as journaling, goal-setting, or mindfulness—is tailored to the client's context. In a decolonised adaptation, these tasks are imbued with cultural meaning. Clients might document oral histories, create a family tree rooted in ancestral wisdom, or attend community gatherings. These practices support identity consolidation and intergenerational healing, particularly among clients affected by forced migration, statelessness, or racial marginalisation (Denborough, 2014; Barghouti, 2000).

6. Experiential Techniques

Pluralistic therapy often employs experiential work such as visualisation, somatic exercises, or role-play. Decolonised therapy embraces these too, but with a focus on cultural embodiment. This might include reconnecting to the body through traditional dance, prayer postures, breathwork grounded in spiritual traditions, or guided imagery that evokes ancestral homelands (Ogden & Fisher, 2015; Ginwright, 2016). These methods affirm that trauma is not only psychological—it is also somatic, historical, and collective.

Divergences Between Pluralistic and Decolonised Frameworks

While there are powerful synergies between the pluralistic approach proposed by McLeod and Cooper and decolonised approaches, their differences highlight the political edge of decolonised practice.

1. Focus on Historical and Structural Power Dynamics

Pluralistic psychotherapy values cultural diversity and client-led direction, but it does not always interrogate the historical and structural conditions that shape mental health. Decolonised therapy, by contrast, explicitly critiques the legacy of colonial psychiatry and its ongoing reproduction through Eurocentric standards (Fernando, 2017; Summerfield, 1999). In this sense, decolonisation is a political project that demands contextualisation, reparative justice, and epistemic accountability (Tuck & Yang, 2012).

2. Cultural Ownership and Ethics

Decolonised practice places significant weight on the origins and ownership of healing practices. It challenges the uncritical borrowing of Indigenous and Global South traditions without proper acknowledgment or understanding. Pluralistic therapy, while integrative, has been critiqued for appropriating techniques without sufficient attention to context or ethics (Moodley & Ocampo, 2014; Smith, 2012). Decolonised frameworks insist that respect, consultation, and redistribution of power accompany any engagement with cultural forms.

3. Political and Collective Healing

Pluralism focuses on individual wellbeing and client-defined outcomes. In contrast, decolonised therapy is deeply attuned to collective healing—especially for communities impacted by colonialism, racial violence, or structural marginalisation (Bryant-Davis, 2019; Prilleltensky, 2003). The therapy room becomes a space not only for personal repair but for communal remembering and resistance.

The pluralistic approach provides a flexible and inclusive framework that resonates deeply with the principles of decolonised psychotherapy. Its emphasis on collaboration, diversity, and cultural responsiveness offers important tools for client-centred practice across a range of settings. However, the explicit focus on historical justice, power analysis, and community resilience ensures that decolonised psychotherapy stands apart as a more radical, transformative practice.

Used with intention and humility, pluralistic tools can support decolonised aims—especially when therapists are willing to critique their own positionality and centre Indigenous, diasporic, and historically marginalised knowledge systems (Martín-Baró, 1994).

In the second half of this chapter, I will turn to clinical examples that demonstrate how pluralistic techniques can be adapted within decolonised frameworks—while reflecting on the tensions, limitations, and possibilities that emerge in this evolving space.

Case Examples: Applying Pluralistic Tools in a Decolonised Context

A fundamental strength of the pluralistic approach is its adaptability to a range of client needs, cultural contexts, and therapeutic goals (Cooper & McLeod, 2011). This adaptability resonates with the core values of decolonised psychotherapy, which honours not only individual narratives but the political and historical landscapes that shape those narratives. When pluralistic methods are situated within a decolonised framework, their application gains deeper ethical relevance by engaging directly with the structural and cultural injustices that influence psychological distress.

Example 1: Reconnecting with Cultural Identity

Consider a client from a diasporic background navigating disconnection from their cultural heritage while adapting to life in Western Europe. A pluralistic therapist might begin with collaborative goal setting, supporting the client's desire to explore identity and belonging. Narrative therapy may be used to reframe the client's migration experience as one of resilience and generational strength (White & Epston, 1990).

However, a decolonised therapist would go further—explicitly naming and validating the systemic forces at play: racism, cultural erasure, and epistemic marginalisation (Kirmayer et al., 2014). Cultural resources—ritual, language, prayer, ancestral connection—would not be seen merely as therapeutic tools but as acts of reclamation. Therapy becomes a space where personal healing and collective memory co-exist.

This approach also considers intergenerational trauma not as inherited pathology, but as the ongoing impact of colonial violence (Gone, 2013; Thomas et al., 2018). In practice, this might mean helping the client reconnect with elders, engage in cultural storytelling, or explore how their survival reflects communal resilience rather than individual struggle.

Example 2: Addressing Workplace Inequities

A second case involves a Black professional seeking therapy due to workplace microaggressions and systemic marginalisation. Within a pluralistic model, the therapist might offer CBT to address internalised stress and assertiveness training to navigate difficult interactions (Cooper & Dryden, 2016).

While these tools may have value, a decolonised perspective reframes the issue. The client's experience is not viewed in isolation but recognised as part of a wider pattern of structural racism embedded in professional environments (Bryant-Davis, 2019; Sue et al., 2007). The therapist does not only focus on adaptation, but also on validation and resistance—creating space to process racial trauma, develop critical consciousness, and explore solidarity-based strategies.

For instance, mindfulness techniques could be adapted through culturally resonant practices—such as African diasporic breathing traditions or grounding rituals rooted in spiritual heritage (Moodley & Ocampo, 2014; Ogden & Fisher, 2015). This shifts therapy from coping to critical engagement with injustice.

A Distinctive Ethical Orientation

Whereas earlier chapters have explored social justice as an ethical foundation for decolonised psychotherapy (see Chapter 4), this section emphasises its therapeutic function—how pluralistic tools can be recast to support liberation, not just symptom relief. While pluralistic therapy honours difference, it does not necessarily interrogate the colonial legacies embedded in psychological practice or institutions (Summerfield, 1999; Smith, 2012).

From Cultural Sensitivity to Structural Awareness

Pluralism may acknowledge racism as a contextual factor; decolonised therapy treats it as a systemic structure requiring active interrogation in the therapy room (Fernando, 2017). This shift matters: it repositions the client not as maladapted but as navigating unjust systems. It also implicates the therapist—calling them into ongoing ethical accountability and solidarity.

For example, a pluralistic therapist supporting a queer client might focus on identity affirmation and coping strategies. A decolonised therapist would add a broader critique of heteronormativity and offer pathways toward collective empowerment—such as connecting the client with LGBTQ+ advocacy networks or incorporating queer cultural forms into the session space (Reynolds, 2019).

Therapy as a Site of Structural Intervention

Decolonised psychotherapy extends beyond the individual—it seeks to transform the therapeutic space itself. This might involve rethinking clinic design, language use, intake forms, and service models to ensure they are inclusive, anti-oppressive, and culturally affirming (Smith, 2012). It may also include engaging in community consultation, participatory action, or advocacy.

Rather than viewing social justice as separate from clinical practice, decolonised therapy insists that justice is therapeutic. It proposes that healing cannot be severed from power, history, and resistance.

Where Decolonised Psychotherapy Goes Beyond the Pluralistic Approach

Although pluralistic psychotherapy offers valuable flexibility and inclusivity, its limitations become clear when contrasted with the deeper structural commitments of decolonised therapy. While both aim to honour diversity and client agency, decolonised psychotherapy incorporates political, historical, and epistemic dimensions that pluralism does not inherently address.

1. Explicit Critique of Colonial Legacies

Pluralistic therapy encourages openness to different methods but remains largely silent on the colonial and Eurocentric foundations of mainstream psychological knowledge (Fernando, 2017; Smith, 2012). In contrast, decolonised psychotherapy makes these legacies explicit, foregrounding the ways colonial violence, racism, and assimilationist ideologies have shaped therapeutic models and pathologised non-Western ways of knowing and healing (Watkins & Shulman, 2008; Summerfield, 1999).

Therapists working within a decolonised framework are encouraged to understand the historical production of knowledge, question universalised models of mental health, and challenge the dominance of Western paradigms in both theory and technique. This orientation insists that healing cannot occur in a vacuum, but must account for the social, political, and historical contexts in which suffering emerges.

2. Focus on Collective Healing

Pluralistic therapy tends to centre the individual client and their therapeutic goals. While this individualised approach is respectful of client autonomy, it can miss the communal and political dimensions of suffering and resilience, particularly for clients from colonised, racialised, or displaced communities (Bryant-Davis, 2019; Kirmayer et al., 2014).

Decolonised therapy expands the frame by locating distress not only within the person but within families, communities, and historical trauma. It engages with collective practices—ritual, intergenerational dialogue, community activism—as therapeutic resources, recognising that individual wellbeing is deeply entangled with social and cultural systems (Martín-Baró, 1994; Mohatt et al., 2014). A client's healing may involve rebuilding cultural continuity, restoring dignity to oppressed histories, or re-establishing broken bonds with land, language, or memory.

3. Therapist Accountability

While pluralistic therapy values collaboration, it does not necessarily require therapists to examine their own positionality. Decolonised psychotherapy demands this self-reflexivity as central to ethical practice. Therapists need to examine their identities, biases, and cultural assumptions—and to reflect on how their presence in the room either reproduces or resists colonial dynamics.

This includes an ongoing commitment to critical self-inquiry: Whose knowledge am I privileging? How might I unintentionally silence or pathologise cultural difference? What do I need to unlearn? Such questions move therapist reflexivity from personal introspection to a political and relational practice.

4. Integration of Traditional Healing Practices

Pluralistic therapy allows for the incorporation of diverse practices, but does not always interrogate the ethics of appropriation. Without critical engagement, this can lead to the superficial use of traditional techniques (e.g. mindfulness, smudging, storytelling) devoid of their cultural, spiritual, or political significance (Tuck & Yang, 2012; Smith, 2012).

In decolonised psychotherapy, the use of traditional healing practices is approached with respect, humility, and accountability. Therapists are expected to seek guidance, collaborate with cultural elders or community leaders, and understand the meaning and origins of the practices they are engaging with. Healing is embedded in relational ethics.

For instance, a decolonised therapist using breathwork with a client from a Buddhist background may acknowledge its spiritual roots and discuss how the practice has been recontextualised in therapy. This ensures that cultural practices are not commodified but honoured (Moodley & Ocampo, 2014).

The Role of Cultural Resources

Both pluralistic and decolonised frameworks recognise the healing potential of cultural resources. However, while pluralism often treats culture as a helpful adjunct to clinical technique, decolonised psychotherapy views cultural practice as central to resistance, survival, and sovereignty (Delgado Bernal, 2002; Gone, 2013).

For example, drumming may be used in a pluralistic session for emotional regulation. In a decolonised framework, the therapist might explore the historical role of drumming as a communal act of resistance during slavery or colonisation. Here, culture is not just therapeutic—it is political, embodied, and ancestral.

Overcoming Challenges in Integration

Integrating pluralistic methods with decolonised ethics holds promise, but it also presents important tensions that require care, skill, and critical awareness.

1. Therapist Training and Competence

Therapists must be trained not only in pluralistic techniques but in the histories of colonialism, racialisation, and cultural trauma that shape client experiences (Hutchings, & Lee-Morgan, 2016; Prilleltensky, 2003). Decolonised practice requires more than cultural competence—it calls for political literacy and cultural humility. This includes engaging with anti-racist frameworks, postcolonial scholarship, and Indigenous epistemologies.

2. Navigating Ethical Dilemmas

The pluralistic emphasis on client preference may risk ethical dilemmas if therapists lack awareness of the deeper significance of cultural practices. For example, a therapist might integrate a sacred practice without understanding its cultural meaning, inadvertently causing harm. Decolonised psychotherapy urges consultation, co-design, and community engagement to avoid such missteps (Fernando, 2017; Moodley & Palmer, 2006).

3. Balancing Individual and Collective Needs

Pluralistic therapy often focuses on client-specific goals, while decolonised frameworks attend to collective liberation. Therapists must navigate the tensions between honouring individual voice and recognising communal, historical wounds. For clients from collectivist or historically marginalised communities, therapy must hold both—the personal and the political, the internal and the relational (Ginwright, 2016).

Conclusion

Pluralistic psychotherapy and decolonised psychotherapy share valuable common ground: both challenge the rigidity of single-school models, affirm cultural diversity, and promote collaboration. However, decolonised psychotherapy extends the conversation, embedding healing within histories of resistance, cultural survival, and structural transformation.

As a practitioner drawing from pluralistic principles, I find my work enriched when informed by decolonised thoughts. This integration invites greater humility, deeper listening, and a more expansive understanding of what healing requires. It allows me to adapt pluralistic tools not only for clinical flexibility, but for ethical and political resonance.

Decolonised psychotherapy reminds us that therapy is never neutral. It is shaped by who we are, where we come from, and what systems we uphold or dismantle. When pluralism is paired with the radical commitments of decolonised work, it becomes more than eclectic—it becomes accountable, liberatory, and transformative.

In the next chapter, I will explore the ethical foundations of this work—focusing on boundaries, accountability, and self-reflexivity as essential pillars of decolonised practice.

References

Barghouti, M. (2000). *I saw Ramallah* (A. Soueif, Trans.). Bloomsbury.

Bryant-Davis, T. (2019). The cultural context of trauma recovery: Considering the posttraumatic stress disorder practice guideline and intersectionality. *American Psychologist, 74*(1), 101–116. 10.1037/pst0000241

Cooper, M., & Dryden, W. (2016). *The handbook of pluralistic counselling and psychotherapy.* Sage.

Cooper, M., & McLeod, J. (2011). *Pluralistic counselling and psychotherapy.* Sage.

Delgado Bernal, D. (2002). Critical race theory, Latino critical theory, and critical raced-gendered epistemologies: Recognizing students of color as holders and creators of knowledge. *Qualitative Inquiry, 8*(1), 105–126. https://doi.org/10.1177/107780040200800107

Denborough, D. (2014). *Retelling the stories of our lives: Everyday narrative therapy to draw inspiration and transform experience.* Norton.

Duran, E. (2006). *Healing the soul wound: Counseling with American Indians and other Native peoples.* Teachers College Press.

Fernando, S. (2017). *Institutional racism in psychiatry and clinical psychology: Race matters in mental health.* Palgrave Macmillan.

Fisher-Borne, M., Cain, J. M., & Martin, S. L. (2015). From mastery to accountability: Cultural humility as an alternative to cultural competence. *Social Work Education, 34*(2), 165–181. https://doi.org/10.1080/02615479.2014.977244

Freire, P. (1970). *Pedagogy of the oppressed.* Continuum.

Ginwright, S. (2016). *Hope and healing in urban education: How urban activists and teachers are reclaiming matters of the heart.* Routledge.

Gone, J. P. (2013). Redressing First Nations historical trauma: Theorizing mechanisms for Indigenous culture as mental health treatment. *Transcultural Psychiatry, 50*(5), 683–706. https://doi.org/10.1177/1363461513487669

Hartmann, W. E., & Gone, J. P. (2016). Psychological-mindedness and American Indian historical trauma: Interviews with service providers from a Great Plains reservation. *American Journal of Community Psychology, 57*(1–2), 229–242. https://doi.org/10.1002/ajcp.12036

hooks, b. (1994). *Teaching to transgress: Education as the practice of freedom.* Routledge.

Huff, R. M., Kline, M. V., & Peterson, D. V. (Eds.). (2014). *Health promotion in multicultural populations: A handbook for practitioners and students* (3rd ed.). Sage Publications.

Hutchings, J., & Lee-Morgan, J. (Eds.). (2016). *Decolonisation in Aotearoa: Education, research and practice*. NZCER Press.

Kirmayer, L. J., Sehdev, M., Whitley, R., Dandeneau, S. F., & Isaac, C. (2014). Community resilience: Models, metaphors and measures. *International Journal of Indigenous Health, 5*(1), 62–117.

Martín-Baró, I. (1994). *Writings for a liberation psychology* (A. Aron & S. Corne, Eds.). Harvard University Press.

Mohatt, N. V., Thompson, A. B., Thai, N. D., & Tebes, J. K. (2014). Historical trauma as public narrative: A conceptual review of how history impacts present-day health. *Social Science & Medicine, 106*, 128–136. https://doi.org/10.1016/j.socscimed.2014.01.043

Moodley, R., & Ocampo, M. (Eds.). (2014). *Critical psychiatry and mental health: Exploring the work of Suman Fernando in clinical practice*. Routledge.

Moodley, R., & Palmer, S. (2006). *Race, culture and psychotherapy: Critical perspectives in multicultural practice*. Routledge.

Ogden, P., & Fisher, J. (2015). *Sensorimotor psychotherapy: Interventions for trauma and attachment*. Norton.

Prilleltensky, I. (2003). Understanding, resisting, and overcoming oppression: Toward psychopolitical validity. *American Journal of Community Psychology, 31*(1–2), 195–201. https://doi.org/10.1023/A:1023043108210

Reynolds, V. (2019). The zone of fabulousness: Resisting vicarious trauma with connection, collective care and justice-doing. *International Journal of Narrative Therapy & Community Work, 2019*(1), 7–16.

Smith, L. T. (2012). *Decolonizing methodologies: Research and Indigenous peoples* (2nd ed.). Zed Books.

Summerfield, D. (1999). A critique of seven assumptions behind psychological trauma programmes in war-affected areas. *Social Science & Medicine, 48*(10), 1449–1462. https://doi.org/10.1016/S0277-9536(98)00450-X

Sue, D. W., Capodilupo, C. M., Torino, G. C., Bucceri, J. M., Holder, A. M. B., Nadal, K. L., & Esquilin, M. (2007). Racial microaggressions in everyday life: Implications for clinical practice. *American Psychologist, 62*(4), 271–286. https://doi.org/10.1037/0003-066X.62.4.271

Tuck, E., & Yang, K. W. (2012). Decolonization is not a metaphor. *Decolonization: Indigeneity, Education & Society, 1*(1), 1–40.

Watkins, M., & Shulman, H. (2008). *Toward psychologies of liberation*. Palgrave Macmillan.

White, M., & Epston, D. (1990). *Narrative means to therapeutic ends*. Norton.

Chapter Eight

Ethics, Boundaries, and Self-Reflexivity

In Decolonised Psychotherapy

"Without reflection, we go blindly on our way, creating more un-intended consequences and failing to achieve anything useful."
— Margaret J. Wheatley

Ethics in psychotherapy has always been considered foundational, but within a decolonised framework, the stakes are immeasurably higher. Decolonised psychotherapy does not merely apply conventional ethical codes—it reconstructs them from the ground up. It invites practitioners to interrogate their assumptions, reflect on their social location, and reimagine therapeutic relationships in light of histories of oppression, power asymmetries, and the ongoing consequences of colonialism (Smith, 2012; Fernando, 2017).

To practise ethically in this space, a therapist must embrace cultural humility, continuous reflexivity, and a willingness to relinquish professional authority where it becomes an obstacle to genuine connection. Ethics is not a static checklist; it is a relational, political, and dynamic process. The aim is not merely to avoid harm but to actively dismantle harm embedded within dominant therapeutic traditions.

This approach demands a shift from therapy as a one-directional encounter to a collaborative and culturally grounded partnership. It begins by recognising that mainstream ethical codes—while well-intentioned—are often rooted in Eurocentric, individualist, and middle-class worldviews. These frameworks may fail to reflect the lived realities of clients whose experiences are shaped by intergenerational trauma, racial injustice, forced displacement, or systemic marginalisation (Adams &

Estrada-Villalta, 2017; Wendt & Gone, 2012). If therapy is to serve as a tool of healing rather than assimilation, its ethical boundaries must be expanded to include justice, dignity, and the restoration of cultural agency.

The Complexity of Informed Consent

In any therapeutic context, informed consent is a foundational ethical practice. Clients must understand the process, goals, and limitations of therapy before they can participate meaningfully. However, in decolonised psychotherapy, informed consent must extend beyond procedural clarity—it must also engage with the philosophical foundations and political commitments of the work.

This means recognising that terms such as "decolonisation" or "colonised mind" may carry unintended emotional and cultural weight. Clients who have internalised dominant narratives of pathology, passivity, or deficiency may perceive these concepts as accusatory rather than liberating. A decolonised therapist must navigate this carefully—not diluting the framework, but translating it in ways that centre empathy and client agency.

For example, imagine a Palestinian professional in London pausing during an early session to ask, "Are you saying there's something wrong with me?" The word *decolonising* felt like an indictment—an implication that he had somehow failed to resist colonial imprints. Rather than sidestepping the discomfort, it can be used as a point of relational deepening. Together, unpack how societal conditioning—not individual fault—has shaped many of his experiences, including the pressure to assimilate, code-switch, and overcompensate in professional spaces. This requires not only linguistic care but also an attuned sensitivity to the emotional politics of language (Chilisa, 2012).

Informed consent in this context is not a one-off agreement—it is a fluid, ongoing negotiation. It involves checking in regularly about how clients are engaging with the framework, and offering space for refusal, resistance, or redefinition. Clients must be invited—not compelled—into this work, with full acknowledgement that readiness is shaped by many factors, including cultural background, past exposure to activism or critical theory, and present psychosocial safety.

For clients unfamiliar with systemic language, the therapist must serve as translator, bridge, and co-explorer, gradually introducing decolonial ideas through the lens of lived experience, relational patterns, and shared storytelling (Gone, 2013; Watkins & Shulman, 2008). At its best, informed consent in a decolonised frame becomes an invitation to reclaim meaning, rather than submit to an imposed narrative.

Reflexivity: The Therapist as an Ongoing Work-in-Progress

Central to ethical practice in decolonised psychotherapy is deep and continuous reflexivity. This goes far beyond cultural awareness or professional reflection—it is an ethic of relational accountability, grounded in the recognition that all therapeutic work is shaped by histories of power, positionality, and privilege (hooks, 1994; Fisher-Borne et al., 2015).

Reflexivity in this context is not introspection for its own sake. It is a discipline that asks: How might my cultural location, training, or worldview limit my understanding of this client's pain or resilience? How might I unintentionally reproduce colonial dynamics in how I speak, interpret, or "treat" someone?

Consider a white European therapist working with a Syrian refugee. Despite a genuine commitment to anti-racist practice, the therapist might unknowingly prioritise individual insight over communal healing, or fail to recognise how certain symptoms (e.g., hypervigilance) are shaped not only by trauma but by surveillance, statelessness, or language barriers. Reflexivity here demands more than technical correction—it requires the therapist to decentre themselves, recognise the limits of their worldview, and allow the client's cultural intelligence to guide the work (Comas-Díaz, 2006).

Reflexivity also includes a willingness to be challenged. In some cases, clients may bring perspectives that directly unsettle the therapist's assumptions. For instance, a Libyan client might express suspicion toward psychological labels, drawing from a history in which psychiatry was used as a colonial or state control mechanism. Rather than dismissing this as "resistance," the therapist must treat it as valuable insight into the sociopolitical context of healing (Mills, 2014).

As Chimamanda Ngozi Adichie reminds us in her TED talk, "The danger of a single story" lies in reducing people to one lens, one script, one diagnosis. Ethical practice in this context is about resisting the impulse to generalise—to reduce a client to a stereotype of their religion, nationality, gender, or trauma history. Instead, the therapist must honour the full complexity of lived experience, and accept that cultural meaning is never static, singular, or predictable.

Power, Boundaries, and Shared Authority

Traditional Western models of psychotherapy often position the therapist as expert—the diagnostician, the interpreter, the fixer. This model reflects not only a clinical hierarchy but an epistemological one, in which psychological knowledge is positioned as superior to embodied, cultural, or community wisdom (Adams & Estrada-Villalta, 2017). Decolonised psychotherapy challenges this structure by reimagining the therapeutic relationship as a space of shared authority. Here, the therapist does not "give" power to the client, but rather recognises that the client already possesses expertise—rooted in their lived experience, cultural worldview, and survival strategies.

This shift from hierarchical to collaborative relationships has profound ethical implications. It compels therapists to relinquish control, embrace mutuality, and reflect on how their training or institutional positioning might obscure or silence client knowledge (hooks, 1994; Wendt & Gone, 2012). Shared authority, however, does not mean the erosion of boundaries or containment. On the contrary, a decolonised frame recognises that clear, negotiated boundaries are essential, especially when working with individuals and communities whose boundaries have been consistently violated by systems of colonisation, displacement, or institutional harm (Smith, 2012; Comas-Díaz, 2006).

A Somali refugee living in Dublin once shared her discomfort with a previous therapist who encouraged her to "speak her truth" prematurely. *"She didn't understand,"* the client said, *"that telling my story to her felt like reliving the trauma all over again."* In this case, the therapist's intention was rooted in a Western value system that equates disclosure with healing. But in many cultures—and for many trauma survivors—healing begins with containment, safety, creating social connections and control over one's own narrative (Denborough, 2014). A decolonised approach would ask: *What does safety look like for this client? Whose pace are we following? And crucially, what assumptions am I carrying about what healing should look like?*

Shared authority also demands attunement to relational ethics—the ability to remain flexible while protecting the emotional boundaries of the client. This includes being transparent about the limits of the therapist's role and holding space for disagreement or resistance without resorting to defensiveness or authority-based correction. In this model, the therapist is not the gatekeeper of healing, but a co-traveller who walks beside the client with cultural humility and critical self-awareness.

The Language of Healing

Language is not neutral—it is political, cultural, and deeply relational. In decolonised psychotherapy, language becomes an ethical site where healing can either be facilitated or obstructed. Words such as "trauma," "self-care," or "boundaries" may carry therapeutic weight in Western contexts, but they may also carry unfamiliar, irrelevant, or even alienating meanings for clients from different cultural traditions (Fernando, 2017; Kirmayer et al., 2009).

For example, the idea of "self-care" may seem empowering in individualist societies, but for a Bangladeshi client from a collectivist, kinship-oriented background, healing may be tied to fulfilling relational obligations or maintaining family honour. In such cases, ethical practice involves translating psychological goals into culturally resonant terms—not diluting the work, but reshaping it with sensitivity to the client's worldview. Self-care in this context can be interpreted as a means of attending to oneself in order to remain helpful and supportive to one's family and loved ones.

Ethical language also includes how therapists engage with resistance, discomfort, or misunderstanding—especially when introducing decolonial concepts. Clients from historically privileged backgrounds may experience discussions of colonialism, whiteness, or systemic violence as unsettling. While discomfort can be a productive part of the process, the therapist's role is not to force insight but to facilitate curiosity and openness, ensuring that these conversations serve the therapeutic alliance rather than disrupt it (Ahmed, 2012; Comas-Díaz, 2006).

In all cases, language should be approached as a shared tool, not a therapist-owned lexicon. This includes being willing to learn from the client's cultural idioms, religious frameworks, or spiritual metaphors—whether those involve dreams, ancestral messages, resistance poetry, or prayer. As Chilisa (2012) argues, decolonising practice requires the use of indigenous meaning-making systems as legitimate sources of psychological insight.

Looking Ahead

Ethical practice in decolonised psychotherapy is not a fixed protocol or a manualised set of procedures. It is an evolving, relational process grounded in humility, responsiveness, and an ethic of justice. It demands that therapists unlearn habits of control, question internalised assumptions about therapeutic "progress," and develop the courage to listen more deeply than they speak.

It also requires holding discomfort—not only the client's, but one's own. As therapists step away from the safety of pre-defined roles, they may encounter uncertainty, ambivalence, or moments of rupture. These moments are not ethical failures; they are opportunities to engage in co-created, culturally meaningful repair (Reynolds, 2019).

This work also redefines the role of boundaries. In a decolonised frame, boundaries are not simply protective—they are ethical sites of negotiation. They involve transparency, consent, cultural attunement, and mutual respect. When therapists view boundaries not as rigid rules but as relational agreements, they can begin to build containers strong enough to hold complexity and difference (Kareem & Littlewood, 1992).

As the chapter continues, we will explore concrete strategies for embedding these ethics into therapeutic practice—through supervision, reflective writing, dialogue with community members, and culturally grounded ethical consultation. But for now, let us remember that ethical therapy is not about mastery. It is about mutual accountability, ongoing curiosity, and the radical humility of not always knowing.

Building Ethical Practice in Action

Building on the foundational principles of ethics, boundaries, and reflexivity discussed earlier, this section delves deeper into the practical challenges and strategies therapists must consider when applying a decolonised framework in real-world practice. It explores how practitioners can ethically navigate power dynamics, cultural dissonance, emotional proximity, and the complex interplay of systemic oppression and resilience. Above all, it reaffirms the therapist's ethical responsibility to adapt their approach to the specific histories, values, and needs of each client—resisting the pull of one-size-fits-all frameworks and universalised notions of psychological health.

Addressing Power Dynamics in Therapy

At the heart of decolonised psychotherapy lies a critical interrogation of power. Traditional therapeutic models, even when collaborative in tone, often implicitly reassert hierarchies of knowledge: the therapist as expert, interpreter, and evaluator. This structure mirrors the colonial logic of knowing—in which expertise is held by the dominant culture, and the Other is studied, assessed, or 'treated' (Adams & Estrada-Villalta, 2017; Fernando, 2017).

A decolonised approach instead redistributes epistemic authority. It views the therapist not as the one who fixes, but as a facilitator of collective insight, where the client's lived experience is treated as central, sacred, and worthy of trust.

However, power dynamics are not confined to the therapeutic dyad; they are embedded in the wider social structures in which therapy takes place. A therapist of privileged racial, gender, class, or citizenship background working with a marginalised client must engage in more than self-awareness. They must adopt an active ethic of redistribution and accountability. This includes recognising that therapy itself may be viewed with suspicion—particularly in communities where medical systems have historically pathologised cultural norms or acted as tools of state violence (Mills, 2014; Smith, 2012).

One effective strategy is transparent positioning. A therapist might acknowledge, gently but clearly:

"As a white therapist, I know there are things I may not fully understand about your experience. I welcome your honesty if something I say doesn't land well, and I will try to listen and learn with humility."

This approach does not solve the power imbalance—but it names it, creating a foundation for more equitable dialogue. Transparency is a form of ethical attunement, not performance; it must be accompanied by active listening, cultural humility, and ongoing self-examination (Fisher-Borne et al., 2015; Comas-Díaz, 2006).

Therapists must also remain alert to microaggressions—subtle, often unintentional statements that invalidate, stereotype, or overlook a client's identity. A statement like "Your English is excellent" may seem innocuous, but to a migrant client, it can echo painful experiences of being othered or patronised. The ethical therapist not only avoids such remarks but also creates an environment where clients feel safe to speak about these harms—comments that may sound like compliments but are, in fact, discriminatory. Such remarks can instil fear of retribution or minimisation (Sue et al., 2007).

Boundaries Reimagined

Boundaries in psychotherapy are essential. They serve to protect emotional safety, maintain clarity of roles, and prevent harm. Yet within a decolonised framework, boundaries must be reimagined to account for cultural meanings, collective identities, and historical violations of trust.

Western psychology has often equated professionalism with emotional distance—asserting that too much warmth or relational closeness threatens objectivity. However, in many non-Western and Indigenous contexts, healing is relational, communal, and reciprocal. A decolonised therapist does not abandon boundaries, but reconceptualises them as culturally responsive agreements, co-negotiated with clients rather than imposed upon them (Kareem & Littlewood, 1992).

For example, in working with a Syrian refugee in Europe, a therapist may find that the client views therapy not as a private intervention but as part of a wider social ecosystem. The client may seek family involvement, reference collective histories, or resist individualistic interpretations of suffering. The decolonised practitioner makes space for this—not by compromising ethical standards, but by broadening the definition of safety. This might involve reflecting on how systemic dislocation shapes the client's sense of vulnerability and working to honour their familial and cultural protective systems within the therapy itself (Gone, 2013; Kirmayer et al., 2009).

Boundaries also intersect with historical and institutional trauma. Clients who have faced racial profiling, detention, state surveillance, or displacement may interpret rigid policies—such as no contact between sessions, or bureaucratic intake forms—as reminders of past exclusion. Flexibility, when ethical and consensual, becomes a gesture of reparation, not a breach of professionalism (Watkins & Shulman, 2008).

Healing is Mutual: Therapist Growth in Decolonised Spaces

A rarely discussed but ethically significant dimension of decolonised psychotherapy is that it can also be healing for the therapist. This truth often goes unspoken in clinical literature, which tends to emphasise neutrality, containment, or avoidance of 'countertransference.' Yet working within decolonised frameworks can allow therapists to reclaim parts of themselves—to revisit cultural roots, unlearn colonial conditioning, and deepen their political consciousness (Ginwright, 2016).

This process must be held ethically. The therapy space is not for the therapist's catharsis—but acknowledging the mutuality of healing can prevent shame, denial, or avoidance. A Palestinian therapist, for instance, may feel personal resonance when hearing an Iraqi client describe occupation, displacement, or longing for ancestral land. Rather than hiding this connection, the therapist can hold it quietly, or—if appropriate—name it gently as shared understanding. In doing so, they model relational authenticity without burdening the client (Reynolds, 2019).

The ethical consideration here is balance: therapists must resist the temptation to centre themselves or seek affirmation from clients. At the same time, denying the emotional labour and transformation that occurs for the therapist risks perpetuating the very disembodied professionalism decolonised work resists. Supervision, peer consultation, and reflective practice are essential tools to process the therapist's own growth without compromising the focus of the work.

The Ethical Use of Language

Language, as previously discussed, is not only a tool of communication but a carrier of worldviews. It reflects assumptions about identity, health, morality, and power. In decolonised psychotherapy, language must be treated as an ethical terrain—not neutral, but shaped by cultural hegemony, imperial legacies, and epistemic privilege (Smith, 2012; Chilisa, 2012).

Therapists are ethically obligated to ask of every word they use: *Whose perspective does this represent? Whose story does it centre? Whose values does it invisibly enforce?* This is particularly important when engaging with clients whose worldviews may have been dismissed or pathologised within mainstream psychological discourse.

Take, for example, the humanistic psychology concept of self-actualisation. While empowering in Western individualist contexts, it may feel dissonant—or even selfish—to clients from collectivist traditions where fulfilment is defined relationally. A Bangladeshi client may express healing through acts of family caregiving or community service rather than through self-directed autonomy. In this context, the therapist must reframe growth in culturally aligned terms—such as the fulfilment of interdependent roles or spiritual duty—without imposing Western ideals of "independence" as normative (Kirmayer et al., 2009; Kareem & Littlewood, 1992).

Another ethical imperative lies in challenging the **internalised colonial narratives** that clients may unknowingly carry. A migrant worker in Ireland describing themselves as a "failure to integrate" reveals more about societal exclusion than personal inadequacy. A decolonised therapist would gently explore alternative framings: What systems have made you feel this way? What strengths have helped you survive and resist? This kind of reframing not only restores dignity but highlights the political nature of psychological suffering (Adams & Estrada-Villalta, 2017; Watkins & Shulman, 2008).

Balancing Cultural Sensitivity with Individuality

Cultural sensitivity is often presented as a cornerstone of ethical practice—but without reflexivity, it can drift into essentialism. Decolonised psychotherapy acknowledges culture not as a static blueprint, but as a living, contested, and intersecting force. Therapists must resist the temptation to reduce clients to their cultural or religious identities, especially when those identities are layered with contradiction, struggle, or change.

A client from a conservative Muslim background may simultaneously draw strength from her faith and critique certain gender norms. A decolonised therapist would not assume conflict or harmony but would approach the tension with openness: *How do you make sense of this? What parts of your cultural world feel nurturing, and which feel restrictive?* This stance not only affirms complexity but refuses the flattening gaze of cultural generalisation (Crenshaw, 1991; Moodley & Ocampo, 2014).

Intersectionality, as articulated by Kimberlé Crenshaw, remains central here. A Syrian queer client is not just Syrian or queer—they are navigating systems of patriarchy, racism, migration, and heteronormativity all at once. Ethical practice in this frame demands cultural humility, not just competence—recognising that identity is fluid, power-laden, and not always externally visible (Fisher-Borne et al., 2015; Comas-Díaz, 2006).

Decolonised Reflexivity as an Ethical Imperative

Reflexivity is not a luxury in decolonised practice—it is an ethical obligation. Therapists must turn their analytical gaze not only inward but upward and outward: upward to interrogate the institutions, training, and diagnostic frameworks that shape their practice; outward to examine the broader sociopolitical systems that frame the client's distress.

Take the pathologisation of anger. In many therapeutic paradigms, anger is something to be managed, tamed, or transcended. Yet, for clients facing racism, colonisation, or gendered violence, anger may be a profoundly ethical response—a declaration of personhood in the face of erasure. The therapist's task is not to suppress this anger but to contextualise it, honour it, and explore how it can be transformed into resistance, meaning-making, or activism (Ginwright, 2016; Bryant-Davis, 2019).

Yet such reframing may provoke discomfort—especially in therapists socialised to avoid conflict or maintain a surface neutrality. Here, reflexivity must move from personal growth to professional accountability. *What emotions am I privileging as therapeutic? What emotions make me withdraw? What norms am I reproducing in my silence?*

A Call to Ethical Action

Ethics in decolonised psychotherapy is not a fixed standard—it is a living practice, a relational stance, and a commitment to justice. It asks therapists not only to do less harm, but to undo the harms that have been normalised by the collusion of psychology with colonial and capitalist structures (Reynolds, 2019).

This includes embracing the vulnerability of not knowing, the courage to unlearn, and the humility to listen when clients critique the therapy itself. It also includes recognising that therapists, too, are human beings situated within oppressive systems—and that therapy can, at times, offer healing to both client and therapist. When held ethically, this mutual transformation is not a boundary violation, but a testament to the shared human stakes of this work (hooks, 1994; Gone, 2013).

As therapists adapt their ethical frameworks to decolonised practice, they must remain vigilant to the risks of appropriation, overidentification, and unconscious re-centring of self. Supervision, cultural consultation, and community accountability are vital not just for support but for ethical integrity.

Closing Reflection

Ethical practice in decolonised psychotherapy is a call to action, not a code of compliance. It is a refusal to treat therapy as neutral or detached. It is an invitation to co-create spaces where both pain and power can be witnessed, where culture is a resource rather than a risk, and where healing is not the restoration of normality but the reclamation of dignity.

As we move into the next chapter, *Limitations of Decolonised Psychotherapy and its Challenges*, we must hold space for complexity. No model is immune from critique, and decolonised practice itself must evolve in response to tensions, contradictions, and blind spots. Ethical therapists are not those who have all the answers, but those who remain open to being changed by the work.

References

Adams, H., & Estrada-Villalta, S. (2017). Decolonizing psychological science: Introduction to the special thematic section. *Journal of Social and Political Psychology, 5*(1), 213–238. https://doi.or g/10.5964/jspp.v5i1.750

Ahmed, S. (2012). *On being included: Racism and diversity in institutional life*. Duke University Press.

Bryant-Davis, T. (2019). The cultural context of trauma recovery: Considering the post_ traumatic stress disorder practice guideline and intersectionality. *American Psychologist, 74*(1), 101–116. 10.1037/pst0000241

Chilisa, B. (2012). *Indigenous research methodologies*. Sage.

Comas-Díaz, L. (2006). Cultural variation in the therapeutic relationship. In J. C. Norcross (Ed.), *Psychotherapy relationships that work* (pp. 81–98). Oxford University Press.

Crenshaw, K. (1991). Mapping the margins: Intersectionality, identity politics, and violence against women of color. *Stanford Law Review, 43*(6), 1241–1299. https://doi.org/10.2307/122 9039

Denborough, D. (2014). *Retelling the stories of our lives: Everyday narrative therapy to draw inspiration and transform experience*. Norton.

Fernando, S. (2017). *Institutional racism in psychiatry and clinical psychology: Race matters in mental health*. Palgrave Macmillan.

Fisher-Borne, M., Cain, J. M., & Martin, S. L. (2015). From mastery to accountability: Cultural humility as an alternative to cultural competence. *Social Work Education, 34*(2), 165–181. https ://doi.org/10.1080/02615479.2014.977244

Ginwright, S. (2016). *Hope and healing in urban education: How urban activists and teachers are reclaiming matters of the heart*. Routledge.

Gone, J. P. (2013). Redressing First Nations historical trauma: Theorizing mechanisms for Indigenous culture as mental health treatment. *Transcultural Psychiatry, 50*(5), 683–706. https: //doi.org/10.1177/1363461513487669

hooks, b. (1994). *Teaching to transgress: Education as the practice of freedom*. Routledge.

Kareem, J., & Littlewood, R. (1992). *Intercultural therapy: Themes, interpretations and practice*. Blackwell Scientific.

Kirmayer, L. J., Sehdev, M., Whitley, R., Dandeneau, S. F., & Isaac, C. (2009). Community resilience: Models, metaphors and measures. *International Journal of Indigenous Health, 5*(1), 62–117.

Mills, C. (2014). *Decolonizing global mental health: The psychiatrization of the majority world.* Routledge.

Moodley, R., & Ocampo, M. (Eds.). (2014). *Critical psychiatry and mental health: Exploring the work of Suman Fernando in clinical practice.* Routledge.

Prilleltensky, I. (2003). Understanding, resisting, and overcoming oppression: Toward psychopolitical validity. *American Journal of Community Psychology, 31*(1–2), 195–201. https://doi .org/10.1023/A:1023043108210

Reynolds, V. (2019). The zone of fabulousness: Resisting vicarious trauma with connection, collective care and justice-doing. *International Journal of Narrative Therapy & Community Work, 2019*(1), 7–16.

Smith, L. T. (2012). *Decolonizing methodologies: Research and Indigenous peoples* (2nd ed.). Zed Books.

Sue, D. W., Capodilupo, C. M., Torino, G. C., Bucceri, J. M., Holder, A. M. B., Nadal, K. L., & Esquilin, M. (2007). Racial microaggressions in everyday life: Implications for clinical practice. *American Psychologist, 62*(4), 271–286. https://doi.org/10.1037/0003-066X.62.4.271

Watkins, M., & Shulman, H. (2008). *Toward psychologies of liberation.* Palgrave Macmillan.

Wendt, D. C., & Gone, J. P. (2012). Decolonizing psychological inquiry in American Indian communities: The promise of qualitative methods. *American Journal of Community Psychology, 50*(3–4), 386–396. https://doi.org 10.1037/13742-009

Chapter Nine

Limitations of Decolonised Psychotherapy

And its Challenges

"*D*ecolonisation is not about erasing the past, but about remembering *it differently and acting on that memory with courage.*" — Vandana Shiva

Decolonised psychotherapy offers a powerful critique of mainstream mental health paradigms, reframing healing through lenses of historical injustice, collective resistance, and cultural reclamation. Yet like all frameworks, it is neither immune to critique nor above reproach. If decolonisation is to remain a living, ethical, and liberatory praxis, it must subject itself to the same critical scrutiny it demands of others.

This chapter explores the challenges, contradictions, and risks embedded within decolonised psychotherapy. It does not offer dismissal, but rather *loyal opposition*—an invitation to interrogate blind spots, resist co-optation, and clarify the tensions inherent in translating radical theory into therapeutic practice. It is also an appeal to avoid sanctifying the concept of decolonisation itself, which—when unexamined—can drift into abstraction, tokenism, or professional branding devoid of structural accountability.

The Complexity of Defining Decolonisation in Practice

One of the central tensions facing the field is the conceptual ambiguity of "decolonisation." In many spaces, the term has become a symbolic placeholder for diversity, equity, or cultural sensitivity. Yet decolonisation, in its radical form, implies the dismantling of colonial logics, hierarchies, and epistemologies (Tuck & Yang, 2012; Maldonado-Torres, 2007). It is not simply about inclusion—it is about systemic transformation, and in some interpretations, even the repatriation of land and power.

In psychotherapy, this becomes particularly difficult to operationalise. What does it mean to decolonise a therapeutic encounter situated within a clinical room governed by state regulation, insurance protocols, Eurocentric training, and institutional funding? Can a profession that emerged from colonial violence ever truly be decolonised—or only reformed?

Many therapists invoke decolonisation rhetorically while continuing to practise within untransformed systems. For instance, a therapist may introduce cultural metaphors or cite Frantz Fanon but still rely on diagnostic categories such as borderline personality disorder or generalised anxiety—labels that remain embedded in Western, individualist, and often pathologising frameworks (Watters, 2010; Summerfield, 2008). These contradictions are not necessarily acts of bad faith; they reflect the structural entanglements in which all clinicians are embedded. Yet to avoid critique is to risk turning decolonisation into an aesthetic—*a stylistic upgrade to conventional therapy rather than a rupture with its colonial foundations.*

Moreover, therapists often draw from decolonial language without examining the ontological claims it carries. Terms like "ancestral healing" or "colonial trauma" are increasingly used in workshops, supervision, and marketing materials. But without accountability to the communities from which such concepts emerge, they risk becoming decontextualised artefacts—commodified fragments of Indigenous or Global South knowledge systems, repurposed for therapeutic consumption (Smith, 2012; Tuhiwai Smith & Tuck, 2019).

Decolonisation, as I defined it in the introduction of this book, is not a metaphor, nor a symbolic gesture—it is a material, political, and psychological imperative. It involves the full recognition that colonised peoples have the right to repatriation, to reclaim the land, resources, and cultural knowledge that were violently stolen or systematically erased. This includes restitution for historical and ongoing harm, alongside the active dismantling of colonial structures that continue to govern everyday life.

True decolonisation demands the restoration of Indigenous and colonised languages, spiritualities, and ways of being—not as relics of the past, but as vital systems of knowledge in the present.

In psychotherapy, this translates to more than integrating "cultural awareness" or rejecting Eurocentric diagnoses. It means actively working to disrupt the colonial logics embedded in the therapeutic space itself: the privileging of Western epistemologies, the assumption of universality in psychological norms, and the erasure of collective memory and resistance. Decolonising psychotherapy involves standing in solidarity with struggles for justice, creating space for clients' ancestral wisdom and political truths, and recognising that healing, for many, must include the recovery of what was stolen—identity, dignity, language, and land.

The Risk of Overreach and Ontological Dissonance

Another key challenge is the ontological gap between Western therapeutic logic and the worldviews of many marginalised communities. While decolonised psychotherapy seeks to bridge this gap, it often remains constrained by the underlying assumptions of Western psychology: that healing occurs through verbal expression, that the individual is the primary unit of intervention, and that insight leads to transformation.

For clients from traditions that view suffering as a communal, spiritual, or political phenomenon, this can create a form of ontological dissonance. The therapist may unwittingly offer cultural validation but continue to impose therapeutic norms incompatible with the client's lived cosmology. A Yemeni client grieving a loss through Quranic recitation and communal prayer may not experience the same psychological meaning from narrative processing or emotional catharsis. In such cases, attempts to "decolonise" therapy may fall short—not for lack of intention, but due to epistemic boundaries that are yet to be fully recognised (Kirmayer et al., 2014; Wendt & Gone, 2012).

In turn, therapists may feel pressure to extend their role beyond ethical limits—offering spiritual guidance, political solidarity, or cultural education for which they are not adequately prepared. While relational warmth and humility are essential, so too is role clarity. The desire to be "all things" to marginalised clients can replicate a saviour dynamic—well-meaning, but ultimately disempowering (Ahmed, 2012; Fernando, 2017).

Co-optation, Tokenism, and the Marketisation of Decolonisation

As the discourse of decolonisation gains traction in academic and therapeutic circles, it increasingly risks being appropriated by the very institutions it seeks to critique. The language of liberation, if unmoored from its political roots, becomes susceptible to professional branding, market appeal, and institutional domestication. This is not merely ironic—it is structurally dangerous.

In mental health settings, decolonisation is sometimes reduced to aesthetic gestures: renaming services, showcasing diverse staff photos, or introducing tokenistic cultural practices without genuine structural change. What emerges is a superficial multiculturalism that equates representation with transformation, diversity with justice (Kothari, 2006). Workshops titled "Decolonising Therapy" are advertised by institutions with extractive hiring practices or histories of racial exclusion. In such contexts, decolonisation becomes a commodity—an ethos that can be packaged, sold, and consumed without any challenge to power relations.

This mirrors what Nancy Fraser (2000) refers to as "the politics of recognition" divorced from redistribution. Marginalised identities are celebrated, but material inequities remain intact. A therapist of colour may be hired to signal inclusion, yet still be underpaid, unsupported, and expected to carry the emotional labour of institutional reform. Similarly, training programmes may offer decolonial modules while maintaining syllabi that remain grounded in Euro-American epistemologies (Bhambra, 2014).

Such co-optation is not always intentional. Often, it emerges from liberal discomfort with structural critique, or from the desire to appear progressive without risking disruption. Yet the effect is the same: a dilution of decolonisation into liberal inclusionism, where it loses its oppositional force and becomes palatable to dominant norms (Nagar, 2014).

Therapists must remain vigilant to how they might unintentionally participate in these dynamics. For instance, a practitioner might attend a training on Indigenous healing practices, adopt select rituals, and incorporate them into their clinical work—without engaging with the ethical, spiritual, and relational dimensions of those practices, or the communities from which they arise (McCormick, 2009; Warne & Lajimodiere, 2015). This is not cultural appreciation; it is epistemic extraction.

True decolonial praxis resists such flattening. It demands not only cultural fluency, but structural accountability—ongoing dialogue with communities, redistribution of resources, and a commitment to remain open to critique. It may mean refusing to brand oneself as a "decolonised therapist" altogether, recognising that decolonisation is not a personal identity but a collective, unfinished political project (Tuck & Yang, 2012).

Cultural Overload and Therapist Burnout

Another limitation, rarely addressed in celebratory accounts of decolonised therapy, is the emotional toll it takes on therapists—particularly those from marginalised communities. The expectation to always show up with insight, clarity, and radical resistance can create what has been termed *cultural over-responsibility* (Singh, 2016). Therapists of colour, or those with lived experience of colonisation, are often expected to both educate and heal—sometimes within systems that do not recognise their labour.

This phenomenon is compounded by institutional isolation, lack of culturally competent supervision, and the burden of navigating clients' trauma while holding their own. A Senegalese therapist supporting migrant survivors of detention, for example, may find their own experiences of displacement activated by the work—yet encounter silence or pathologisation when seeking support from predominantly Western colleagues (Al-Krenawi & Graham, 2000). In such cases, the therapist becomes both a healer and a hidden site of harm.

The ethics of care, therefore, must extend to therapists themselves. Decolonised psychotherapy must not only challenge oppressive systems, but also reconfigure how care work is distributed, valued, and sustained.

This includes collective supervision models, political solidarity, and institutional restructuring that affirms the humanity of those delivering the care (Mehrotra, 2016).

Reflective Interlude: Between Praxis and Performance

Before proceeding, it is worth pausing to reflect on the tensions outlined so far. The risk of turning decolonisation into a symbolic performance—rather than a radical, accountable practice—is not theoretical. It is happening in real time across disciplines, and psychotherapy is no exception. Below is a summary of key risks and questions raised in this chapter so far:

Table 9.1 Key Tensions in the Misuse and Dilution of Decolonisation in Psychotherapy

Tension	Risk	Decolonial Response
Conceptual ambiguity	Dilution of decolonisation into "diversity" language	Re-anchor in anti-colonial, systemic analysis
Marketisation and branding	Selling "decolonisation" as a credential	Refuse commodification; prioritise community over capital
Institutional tokenism	Inclusion without redistribution	Demand structural change alongside representation
Cultural extraction	Using practices without context or consent	Engage relationally and with ethical humility
Emotional over-responsibility	Therapist burnout and isolation	Collective care and reflective supervision

Capitalism and the Commodification of Healing

These dilemmas are not incidental—they are structurally reinforced by capitalism itself. The commodification of therapy is part of a larger logic: that everything, including care, trauma, identity, and even resistance, can be packaged, marketed, and sold (Illouz, 2008; Davies, 2017). Traditional psychotherapy, despite its therapeutic aspirations, has often functioned as a market-aligned enterprise, reinforcing the consumer logic of paying for personal transformation.

In this model, clients become consumers; therapists become service providers; healing becomes a product. This neoliberal frame is antithetical to the liberatory aims of decolonised practice, which situates healing as relational, communal, and unbounded by transactional ethics. It is no coincidence that the most "popular" forms of therapy in Western markets are those that promise short-term, measurable, individual results—CBT, solution-focused therapy—while more relational, cultural, or political approaches are marginalised (Rose, 1999; Watkins & Shulman, 2008).

The task of decolonised psychotherapy is not to compete in this market, but to challenge the premise. To do so, we must interrogate not only the politics of knowledge but the economics of care. Who profits from the current system? Who is excluded? What might therapy look like when removed from capitalist demands of productivity, efficiency, and growth?

The Problem of Purism: Can We Ever Fully Decolonise Psychotherapy?

A final tension worth naming is the danger of decolonial purism—the belief that therapy must be completely free from Western influence to be valid. While this may sound appealing, it is often unworkable. Most therapists practising today, including those engaged in decolonial work, are trained within Western institutions. They use Western tools, speak in Western professional idioms, and operate within licensure systems built on Western legal frameworks. To imagine a fully decolonised practice divorced from these conditions is, for many, politically aspirational but pragmatically constrained (Ndlovu-Gatsheni, 2013).

Moreover, some Western approaches—such as narrative therapy, parts work, or trauma-informed care—can be *re-appropriated* in ethically responsible ways, especially when adapted with community input and cultural grounding. The goal is not total rejection, but critical integration. The test of decolonial integrity is not whether a therapist avoids all Western influence, but whether they remain accountable to the histories, power dynamics, and cultural meanings their tools invoke (Chilisa, 2012; Moodley & Palmer, 2006).

There is also a risk of shaming therapists who are doing their best within compromised systems—particularly those from historically marginalised communities. A decolonial purism that becomes elitist, rigid, or inaccessible may reproduce the very hierarchies it seeks to dismantle. What is needed instead is a pluralistic, reflexive, and relational ethic—one that holds complexity, permits imperfection, and sees decolonisation as a process, not a destination (Fanon, 1963).

Reflections on the Edge of the Work

As I write this chapter, I am increasingly aware that decolonised psychotherapy is not only a method or critique—it is also a deeply personal, vulnerable, and sometimes conflicted position to inhabit. It asks me to question my training, challenge my affiliations, and sit with the contradictions of practising within systems I wish to transform. I do not write from a place of finality or certainty, but from within the ongoing struggle to live and work with integrity under conditions that are far from ideal.

There are moments—especially in politically charged clinical spaces—when I find myself asking: *Am I doing enough? Am I unconsciously reinforcing harm by working within this institution?* And at other times, I feel the pressure to perform a decolonial purity that is both unrealistic and alienating. These inner tensions are not signs of failure, but signs that I am still listening, still unlearning. I believe that therapists engaging in this work must hold space for ambiguity, without abandoning their principles or pretending neutrality.

What I hope readers take from this chapter is not a blueprint, but an *invitation*. An invitation to ask better questions, to listen harder to those at the margins, and to honour the discomfort that comes with dismantling cherished ideas. Decolonised psychotherapy cannot be formulaic. It is not a new school of therapy, but a politicised ethical stance—one that demands courage, humility, and deep relational accountability.

Conclusion: Imperfection as a Principle, Accountability as a Practice

To engage in decolonised psychotherapy is to work with a framework that is both radical and fragile—full of potential, but vulnerable to distortion. This chapter has explored the tensions that emerge when critical theory meets clinical practice: the risks of commodification, tokenism, conceptual drift, burnout, and purism. These limitations are not reasons to abandon the work. They are reasons to deepen it.

True decolonial practice is not about grand gestures or perfect fluency; it is about staying in the struggle. It is about centring those most harmed by dominant systems, not as metaphors or clients, but as knowledge-holders and co-authors of change. It is about humility without paralysis, action without appropriation, and vision without dogma.

Decolonised psychotherapy must evolve—not by aspiring to completeness, but by remaining responsive, porous, and accountable. In doing so, it can resist the gravitational pull of mainstream absorption and hold open a space for something more courageous: a relational, imperfect, and ethically radical healing practice that makes room for truth, tension, and transformation.

As we move into the next chapter, we continue this journey—not in closure, but in inquiry. What is the path forward for this work, and who gets to decide it?

References

Al-Krenawi, A., & Graham, J. R. (2000). Cultural sensitivity in social work practice with Arab clients in mental health settings. *Health & Social Work, 25*(1), 9–22. https://doi.org/10.1093/hsw/25.1.9

Ahmed, S. (2012). *On being included: Racism and diversity in institutional life.* Duke University Press.

Bhambra, G. K. (2014). *Connected sociologies.* Bloomsbury.

Chilisa, B. (2012). *Indigenous research methodologies.* Sage.

Davies, W. (2017). *The limits of neoliberalism: Authority, sovereignty and the logic of competition.* Sage.

Fanon, F. (1963). *The wretched of the earth* (C. Farrington, Trans.). Grove Press.

Fernando, S. (2017). *Institutional racism in psychiatry and clinical psychology: Race matters in mental health.* Palgrave Macmillan.

Fraser, N. (2000). Rethinking recognition. *New Left Review, 3,* 107–120.

Illouz, E. (2008). *Saving the modern soul: Therapy, emotions, and the culture of self-help.* University of California Press.

Kirmayer, L. J., Sehdev, M., Whitley, R., Dandeneau, S. F., & Isaac, C. (2014). Community resilience: Models, metaphors and measures. *International Journal of Indigenous Health, 5*(1), 62–117.

Kothari, U. (2006). An agenda for thinking about 'race' in development. *Progress in Development Studies, 6*(1), 9–23. https://doi.org/10.1191/1464993406ps124oa

McCormick, R. (2009). Aboriginal approaches to counselling. In L. Kirmayer & G. Guthrie Valaskakis (Eds.), *Healing traditions: The mental health of Aboriginal peoples in Canada* (pp. 337–354). UBC Press.

Mehrotra, G. (2016). *Toward a continuum of intersectionality theorizing for feminist social work scholarship. Affilia, 31*(2), 147–158. https://doi.org/10.1177/0886109910384190

Maldonado-Torres, N. (2007). On the coloniality of being: Contributions to the development of a concept. *Cultural Studies, 21*(2–3), 240–270.

Moodley, R., & Palmer, S. (2006). *Race, culture and psychotherapy: Critical perspectives in multicultural practice.* Routledge.

Nagar, R. (2014). *Muddying the waters: Coauthoring feminisms across scholarship and activism.* University of Illinois Press.

Ndlovu-Gatsheni, S. J. (2013). *Coloniality of power in postcolonial Africa: Myths of decoloniza tion*. Codesria.

Rose, N. (1999). *Governing the soul: The shaping of the private self*. Free Association Books.

Singh, A. A. (2016). *The racial healing handbook: Practical activities to help you challenge privilege, confront systemic racism, and engage in collective healing*. New Harbinger Publications.

Tuck, E., & Yang, K. W. (2012). Decolonization is not a metaphor. *Decolonization: Indigeneity, Education & Society, 1*(1), 1–40.

Tuhiwai Smith, L., & Tuck, E. (2019). *Indigenous and decolonizing studies in education: Map ping the long view*. Routledge.

Warne, D., & Lajimodiere, D. (2015). American Indian health disparities: Psychosocial influ ences. *Social and Personality Psychology Compass, 9*(10), 567–579.

Watkins, M., & Shulman, H. (2008). *Toward psychologies of liberation*. Palgrave Macmillan.

Watters, E. (2010). *Crazy like us: The globalization of the American psyche*. Free Press.

Wendt, D. C., & Gone, J. P. (2012). Decolonizing psychological inquiry in American Indian communities: The promise of qualitative methods. In D. K. Nagata, L. Kohn-Wood, & L. A. Suzuki (Eds.), *Qualitative strategies for ethnocultural research* (pp. 161–178). American Psychological As sociation. https://doi.org/10.1037/13742-009

Chapter Ten

The Path Forward

Decolonising Systems, Minds, and Practice

" The world needs to be reinvented... It can only be reinvented with consciousness. " — Etel Adnan

If decolonised psychotherapy is to be more than a countercultural whisper in a profession still shaped by empire, this chapter must make its intentions plain: the time for symbolic reform is over. What we need now is structural unmaking—of the institutions that train us, the systems that credential us, the psychological models that erase us, and the internalised logics that colonise not only our clients' minds, but our own.

This is not a conclusion, but a beginning. The previous chapters have excavated the foundations—revealing how colonialism, capitalism, and epistemic violence continue to structure what we call mental health. Now, we turn our gaze to action: What must be done to unlearn, dismantle, and reconstruct? Where do we direct our energy so that this work is not merely reflective, but revolutionary?

From Awareness to Architecture: Systems Must Change

At the institutional level, many mental health organisations and training institutions still operate with a white-centred, middle-class, Euro-American epistemology at their core. Diversity panels are offered without power analysis. Race is discussed without empire. Culture is included without colonial history. The result? A therapeutic system that *appears* inclusive but replicates colonial dynamics under the guise of professionalism.

What is required is nothing less than the decolonisation of training curricula. This involves:

- **Embedding anti-colonial histories** into core clinical modules—not as electives, but as foundational knowledge.

- **Challenging DSM-centred diagnostic paradigms** that individualise distress while ignoring state violence, displacement, and structural poverty.

- **Including Indigenous, African, Arab, Asian, Global South and others psychologies** not as supplementary, but as epistemic equals—each rooted in distinct ontologies of healing, relationship, and mind.

Decolonisation here means rejecting the false neutrality of Western models and recognising that all psychology is political. There is no value-free therapy. There are only systems that either reproduce harm—or interrupt it.

Colleges, Conferences, and Credentials: Gatekeeping Must End

Educational institutions and accreditation boards function as gatekeepers of legitimacy. Who is deemed a "qualified" therapist? Whose methods are allowed into the room? In most regions, these answers are still shaped by white Western norms. Even when cultural diversity is acknowledged, it is often managed rather than truly integrated. The decolonisation of credentialing bodies must begin with:

- **Diversifying accreditation panels and exam boards** to include scholars and practitioners with lived, not only academic, experience.

- **Revising ethical codes** to explicitly name power, whiteness, and colonial legacies as ethical concerns—not just cultural "competencies".

- **Creating alternative routes to qualification** for therapists trained in community-based or traditional healing systems that do not fit the Eurocentric mould.

If these changes are not made, then the profession will continue to reward those who assimilate, while punishing those who bring different knowledge systems into the room.

Decolonising the Therapist's Mind: Unlearning as Praxis

While institutional reform is critical, no transformation is complete without internal restructuring. The therapist's own mind—shaped by social location, training, and culture—is one of the most powerful sites of colonisation. It is also one of the most vital frontlines of resistance.

Therapists are trained, often implicitly, to think in binaries: healthy/unhealthy, rational/irrational, insight/defence. These binaries are rarely neutral; they are steeped in colonial, patriarchal, and capitalist values about what it means to be well, to be healed, or to be sane (Mills, 2014). To decolonise the therapist's mind is to challenge the very roots of what we have been taught to consider objective truth.

This unlearning is neither comfortable nor linear. It requires:

- **Acknowledging the psychological inheritance of whiteness**, including internalised superiority, fragility, or saviourism (DiAngelo, 2018; Matias, 2016).

- **Recognising how Eurocentric training has shaped our clinical gaze**—often pathologising behaviours outside the white, individualistic norm.

- **Learning to sit with not-knowing**, and with forms of truth that resist academic codification—ritual, silence, ancestral knowledge, and collective memory.

For example, many therapists are taught that neutrality is ethical. But in contexts of oppression, neutrality can become violence. When a client experiences racism or displacement and the therapist responds with clinical detachment, the silence does not protect—it erases.

To truly practise ethically, therapists must begin asking: *Whose safety am I protecting when I stay silent? Whose voice am I silencing when I speak as an expert?*

Healing the Coloniser's Mind

This project must also include a more difficult and often neglected aim: the decolonisation of the coloniser's psyche. As argued in the book's introduction, the psychological architecture of colonialism lives not only in its victims but in its architects and beneficiaries. These are the minds that have been trained to dominate, extract, and dehumanise—often without recognising themselves as such.

In the therapy room, this means that white therapists, and therapists from historically dominant groups, must not only learn about others—they must learn about themselves in relation to power. This is not about shame or guilt. It is about ethical responsibility and transformation.

What does this look like in practice?

- Engaging in **critical reflexivity**, not only about culture but about *history*, *property*, *violence*, and *entitlement.*

- Creating space in supervision and peer dialogue to explore **internalised superiority or unconscious hierarchy.**

- Learning to **receive feedback from marginalised clients without defensiveness** and to understand that discomfort is not harm, but part of the work.

Decolonising the coloniser's mind is essential—not only for the sake of ethical practice, but because a safer world cannot be built on unexamined power. The future of psychotherapy depends on whether therapists can become both healers and students of their own complicity.

Reimagining Psychotherapy: Concrete Calls to Action

The future of psychotherapy—if it is to be ethical, relevant, and liberatory—must be radically reimagined. Not incrementally tweaked. Not softly rebranded. But restructured at every level: institutionally, pedagogically, interpersonally, and internally.

The following are not recommendations, but imperatives—urgent, necessary shifts for those committed to decolonised healing.

1. Rebuild from the Roots

Stop adding decolonial content as afterthoughts. Redesign training from the ground up. Every therapist-in-training should understand:

- The psychiatric legacies of colonialism and race science.

- The cultural specificity—and limitations—of dominant psychological frameworks.

- The existence of *multiple psychologies*, each grounded in distinct ontologies of healing.

2. Refuse Neutrality

Silence and neutrality uphold power. Therapists must:

- Speak explicitly about colonialism, racism, capitalism, and patriarchy in the room when relevant.

- Learn to name power without fearing the loss of professionalism.

- Recognise that safety and comfort are not the same—and that safety is not evenly distributed.

3. Protect Cultural Integrity

Avoid appropriation in the name of "integration." Therapists must:

- Credit the cultural and spiritual lineages of the practices they use.

- Build relationships with communities whose traditions they engage with.

- Ask consent of the cultures—not only the individuals—being drawn from.

4. Disrupt the Economics of Care

Challenge the commodification of mental health. This means:

- Advocating for publicly funded, culturally responsive services.

- Creating sliding scale or community-led therapy models.

- Valuing healing as a relational right—not a marketable commodity.

5. Stay in the Work

Decolonisation is not an identity or a destination. It is an ongoing practice. Stay reflexive. Stay relational. Stay accountable. Learn. Unlearn. Repeat. And when critique comes, meet it with curiosity, not fragility.

Final Words: A Shared Future

This book has made many demands—of systems, of therapists, of myself and perhaps of you. It has called for the deconstruction of long-held truths, the reconfiguration of clinical norms, and the rehumanisation of therapeutic spaces. But, beneath these critiques is a quieter hope: that healing is still possible. That people can change. That structures can be rebuilt. And that those of us in this profession—when guided by courage, humility, and solidarity—can become part of the transformation.

To decolonise psychotherapy is not to perfect it. It is to make it more human, more honest, and more just. This is the path forward. The rest is up to us.

References

Adnan, E. (2005). *In the heart of the heart of another country*. City Lights Books.

Bhugra, D., & Bhui, K. (2007). Culture and mental health: A comprehensive textbook. *Hodder Arnold*.

Chilisa, B. (2012). *Indigenous research methodologies*. Sage.

DiAngelo, R. (2018). *White fragility: Why it's so hard for white people to talk about racism*. Beacon Press.

Fanon, F. (1963). *The wretched of the earth* (C. Farrington, Trans.). Grove Press.

Fernando, S. (2017). *Institutional racism in psychiatry and clinical psychology: Race matters in mental health*. Palgrave Macmillan.

Hickling, F. W., & Hutchinson, G. (2000). Beyond psychotherapy: Caribbean cultural psychiatry. *Psychiatry, 63*(4), 307–319. https://doi.org/10.1521/psyc.63.4.307.42817

Kirmayer, L. J., & Pedersen, D. (2014). Toward a new architecture for global mental health. *Transcultural Psychiatry, 51*(6), 759–776. https://doi.org/10.1177/1363461514557202

Kumar, D. (2012). *Islamophobia and the politics of empire*. Haymarket Books.

Matias, C. E. (2016). *Feeling white: Whiteness, emotionality, and education*. Sense Publishers.

McKittrick, K. (2015). *Sylvia Wynter: On being human as praxis*. Duke University Press.

Mills, C. (2014). *Decolonizing global mental health: The psychiatrization of the majority world*. Routledge.

Moodley, R., & Palmer, S. (Eds.). (2006). *Race, culture and psychotherapy: Critical perspectives in multicultural practice*. Routledge.

Ndlovu-Gatsheni, S. J. (2013). *Coloniality of power in postcolonial Africa: Myths of decolonization*. Codesria.

Rose, N. (1999). *Governing the soul: The shaping of the private self*. Free Association Books.

Said, E. W. (1978). *Orientalism*. Pantheon Books.

Smith, L. T. (2012). *Decolonizing methodologies: Research and Indigenous peoples* (2nd ed.). Zed Books.

Tuck, E., & Yang, K. W. (2012). Decolonization is not a metaphor. *Decolonization: Indigeneity, Education & Society, 1*(1), 1–40.

Tuhiwai Smith, L., & Tuck, E. (2019). *Indigenous and decolonizing studies in education: Mapping the long view*. Routledge.

Watkins, M., & Shulman, H. (2008). *Toward psychologies of liberation*. Palgrave Macmillan.

Wynter, S. (2003). Unsettling the coloniality of being/power/truth/freedom. *The New Centennial Review, 3*(3), 257–337.

Glossary of Key Terms

The language of decolonisation is rich, evolving, and often grounded in specific political, cultural, and historical contexts. This glossary is offered not as a fixed dictionary, but as a companion to deepen engagement with the ideas presented in this book. Some terms have contested meanings; others carry particular weight in certain communities. Use these definitions as starting points—for reflection, for dialogue, and for further learning. As with decolonised psychotherapy itself, meaning is always co-created.

Ancestral Knowledge

Ways of knowing, healing, and relating passed down through generations—often through oral tradition, ritual, and spiritual practice. Central to decolonised therapy as a counter to Western epistemologies.

Coloniality

The ongoing structures and mindsets of colonial power that persist beyond formal colonisation, shaping institutions, language, and psychology.

Cultural Agency

The ability of individuals and communities to define, reclaim, and live their identities without erasure or assimilation. A goal of decolonised therapeutic practice.

Cultural Extraction

The appropriation of Indigenous or non-Western practices (e.g., smudging, breathwork) without proper context, consent, or accountability.

Decoloniality

A framework for resisting colonial logics and re-centering Indigenous and Global South epistemologies, ontologies, and ways of being.

Decolonised Psychotherapy

A political and ethical stance that critiques the colonial roots of Western mental health systems and centres relational, communal, and culturally sovereign healing practices.

Epistemic Violence

The silencing, erasure, or delegitimisation of entire knowledge systems—often through the dominance of Western science or psychology.

Eurocentrism

A worldview that centres European norms, values, and history as universal or superior, often marginalising other cultural perspectives.

Healing Justice

A collective framework that combines personal healing with social transformation, particularly for communities impacted by oppression.

Intersectionality

A framework coined by Kimberlé Crenshaw that examines how systems of oppression (e.g., racism, sexism, classism) intersect and compound in people's lives.

Marketisation of Therapy

The transformation of healing into a commodified service, often prioritising profitability, efficiency, and consumer satisfaction over community care and cultural relevance.

Neutrality Myth

The belief that therapists can or should remain detached from political or cultural realities. Challenged in decolonised frameworks as a form of complicity.

Ontological Dissonance

The tension between a client's worldview and the assumptions embedded in Western psychotherapy (e.g., individualism, verbal expression, pathologisation).

Othering

The process of defining people as fundamentally different or inferior, often to justify exclusion, surveillance, or control.

Positionality

The therapist's social, cultural, and political location, which shapes how they see the world and engage with clients. Acknowledging this is key to ethical, decolonial practice.

Reflexivity

The ongoing practice of examining one's own assumptions, power, and impact in therapeutic work—especially important for those in positions of privilege.

Structural Violence

Systemic harm embedded in institutions and social norms (e.g., racism, poverty, surveillance) that impact mental health far beyond the individual.

Tokenism

Superficial inclusion of marginalised people or ideas to appear diverse without meaningful structural change or redistribution of power.

Unchilding

A concept describing how racialised children are denied innocence, protection, and empathy—treated as adult, criminal, or threatening. A crucial concept in your intersectional analysis.

Appendices

Usage Notice for Appendices

The tools and resources provided in the appendices of this book are intended to support therapists, supervisors, and mental health professionals who have purchased *Decolonised Minds: When Radical Becomes Rational* by Talha AlAli. These materials may be used freely in personal practice, supervision, and client work for non-commercial purposes.

In addition, practical worksheets and other supporting resources are available online at: https://decolonisedminds.ie/store.

However, any reproduction, distribution, or incorporation of these tools into formal training, workshops, lectures, or institutional programmes—whether for free or for profit—requires prior **written permission** from the author.

To request permission or discuss collaboration, please contact: **press@ decolonisedminds.ie**

Thank you for respecting the integrity and intent of this work.

— *Talha AlAli*

Appendix 1: Therapist Privilege Inventory Tool

Holding the Mirror: A Therapist's Privilege Inventory for Decolonial Practice

Purpose:

To help psychotherapists reflect on the **visible and invisible privileges** they bring into the therapy room—and how these may shape power dynamics, interpretations, and relational safety.

When to Use:

- Before working with clients from different sociocultural or political backgrounds.

- As a monthly reflective supervision tool.

- Prior to intake or assessment with clients facing systemic oppression (e.g. refugees, BIPOC youth, incarcerated individuals).

- During continuing education or training in decolonial or anti-oppressive therapy.

INSTRUCTIONS

- Use this tool individually or in supervision.

- Rate each section optionally (1 = unaware, 5 = fully conscious and accountable).

- Reflect honestly—this is a non-shaming tool for growth, not performance.

Structure: Five Sections

Each section includes **reflection prompts** + **a rating scale** (Optional: 1 = unaware, 5 = fully conscious and accountable).

SECTION 1: Sociocultural Identity Awareness

Reflect on your identities and how they intersect with systems of power.

- What is my racial/ethnic identity and how is it read in this context?

- What is my citizenship or residency status?

- What language(s) do I speak fluently and what languages are deemed "professional" in my field?

- Do I share any of the client's cultural or spiritual practices—or do I assume I understand them?

- What is my class background—how did my family talk about work, wealth, or struggle?

Optional Score (1–5): How clearly am I aware of how these identities give me social power in relation to this client?

SECTION 2: Positional Privileges in the Therapy Room

Acknowledge professional and systemic power you hold *within* the therapeutic space.

- Who controls the time, pace, and content of our sessions—me or the client?

- Do I name and challenge the clinical language I use when it might override the client's narrative?

- Have I openly discussed power differences or invited the client to challenge my interpretations?

- Have I ever asked, "How does my identity or training affect your comfort here?"

Optional Score (1–5): How consistently do I name and negotiate my power with clients?

SECTION 3: Structural Access and Safety

Examine how your **daily safety and access** contrasts with that of your client.

- Can I freely move between countries, borders, or state systems? What documents make that possible?

- Do I trust institutions like police, healthcare, or courts to protect me?

- Am I at risk of surveillance, detention, deportation, or discrimination in this space? Is my client?

- Do I have access to housing, clean water, legal protection, and basic resources?

Optional Score (1–5): How deeply have I considered the client's experience of structural safety vs mine?

SECTION 4: Clinical Assumptions and Norms

Interrogate the theoretical frameworks and models you have been trained in.

- Do I assume insight, verbal disclosure, or emotional expression as markers of "progress"?

- Have I pathologised cultural grief, spirituality, or resistance (e.g., calling righteous anger "dysregulation")?

- Have I adapted my methods to include the client's cultural practices (e.g. prayer, ritual, storytelling)?

- Do I treat Western models (CBT, psychodynamic) as default or as one option among many?

Optional Score (1–5): How critically do I reflect on the cultural assumptions within my therapeutic tools?

SECTION 5: Accountability and Action

Awareness is not enough. What actions do you take to redistribute power and repair harm?

- Have I made space for clients to correct me—verbally or nonverbally?

- Have I ever apologised for a clinical misstep rooted in bias or assumption?

- Have I advocated for community-based or non-Western healing practices?

- Do I use my privilege to challenge institutional harm (e.g., diagnosis bias, access barriers, carceral practices)?

Optional Score (1–5): How often do I turn reflection into accountable action?

Reflection Summary (Optional)

- What surprised me?

- What do I want to learn more about?

- What am I committed to changing?

Might adapt this tool into:

- A workshop activity (breakout discussion)

- A reflective supervision template

Appendix 2: Decolonial Language Audit for Clinical Notes

A Tool for Anti-Oppressive, Culturally Humble, and Child-Honouring Practice

Purpose

To help therapists reflect on the language they use in clinical notes, assessments, reports, and supervision—particularly when working with clients from racialised, colonised, or marginalised communities. This audit supports a shift from medicalised, Eurocentric, and pathologising terminology toward narrative-respecting, relationally grounded, and justice-oriented clinical writing.

Core Question:

Does my language serve the client's healing—or does it reinforce colonial, racialised, or adultifying narratives?

Instructions

- Use this checklist during or after writing clinical notes.

- Apply to case formulations, discharge summaries, progress notes, or assessments.

- Can be used individually or in supervision.

SECTION 1: Naming Power and Context

- Have I acknowledged the systemic roots of this client's distress (e.g., housing crisis, racial discrimination, migration trauma)?

- Am I framing trauma as a reaction to structural violence—not simply as an internal deficit?

- Have I named state, institutional, or historical factors if they shape this client's current situation?

Examples: Problematic: Client exhibits signs of generalised anxiety disorder."

Improved: "Client lives in a hotel with three children and is facing eviction—her symptoms appear linked to prolonged housing precarity that is causing her anxiety."

SECTION 2: Language of Resistance vs Pathology

- Have I considered if this behaviour is a survival strategy—not a symptom?

- Am I framing silence, anger, or mistrust as possible resistance rather than "non-compliance"?

- Have I avoided moralistic or clinical shorthand (e.g., manipulative, attention-seeking, poor insight)?

Examples: Problematic: "Client is resistant to engagement."
Improved: "Client has expressed mistrust of professionals, shaped by past negative encounters with social services."

SECTION 3: Unchilding and Racial Bias

- Am I unconsciously adultifying Black, Brown, Traveller, or migrant children by attributing intent or maturity beyond their age?

- Have I avoided labelling emotional expressions in racialised children as aggression or defiance?

Do I allow space for cultural grief, collective identity, or spiritual expression in my formulations of young people?

Examples: Problematic: "10-year-old male was aggressive and threatening to staff."

Improved: "Client expressed distress by yelling and throwing objects after being separated from his mother in unfamiliar surroundings."

SECTION 4: Voice and Ownership

- Whose voice is centred in this note—mine or the client's?

- Have I included direct quotes where possible to preserve the client's framing of their experience?

- Have I invited the client (when appropriate) to review or co-author summaries or formulations?

Examples: Problematic: "Client denies any trauma."

Improved: "Client said: 'I don't call it trauma. I just had to keep going.'"

SECTION 5: Cultural and Linguistic Framing

- Am I using Western psychological terms without checking whether the client uses similar words or understands them the same way?

- Have I translated the client's culturally grounded expressions into clinical language that distorts or erases their meaning?

- Did I explore what this emotion or experience is called in the client's mother tongue or tradition?

Examples: Problematic: "Client is experiencing hallucinations."
Improved: "Client described hearing her grandmother's voice during prayer, which she understands as spiritual connection, not illness."

SECTION 6: Diagnostic Labels and Institutional Consequences

- Is the diagnosis I have used going to serve this client—or might it lead to surveillance, institutionalisation, or harm?

- Have I critically evaluated the long-term impact of labelling, especially for children of colour and those in care systems?

- Could I have framed this in relational or environmental terms instead of diagnostic ones?

Examples: Problematic: "Client meets criteria for oppositional defiant disorder."
Improved: "Client shows heightened reactivity to adult authority, which may reflect school-based racial profiling and disciplinary trauma."

SECTION 7: Institutional Accountability

- Is this note written with an awareness that it may be read by social workers, judges, or immigration officers?

- Have I protected the client's dignity while fulfilling institutional requirements?

- Have I named systemic failures where relevant rather than allowing client blame to dominate the narrative?

Examples: Problematic: "Client failed to follow through with agreed plan."

Improved: "Client was unable to attend follow-up due to lack of transport reimbursement and work conflict."

Summary Prompts for Reflection

- What dominant narratives did I default to in this note—and why?

- What language could I replace to better reflect the client's worldview and truth?

- Who benefits from how I have described this client—and who is at risk?

- How can I revise this note to be more accurate, ethical, and liberatory?

Closing Thought:

Clinical documentation is not neutral. It shapes access, risk, visibility, and justice. The words we choose either reinforce systems of oppression or make space for healing, truth, and dignity. Let us choose with care.

Use this audit before signing off on reports. Revisit it quarterly to track your evolving language. Share with colleagues to support culture change.

Appendix 3: Structural Humility Reflection Cards

A Tool for Supervision, CPD, and Self-Awareness in Psychotherapy

Purpose

To help therapists reflect on how structural systems—such as housing, immigration, health, education, policing, and childcare—intersect with therapy and shape client experience. These cards are designed to encourage critical self-inquiry, challenge unconscious alignments with oppressive systems, and support ethical, decolonial, and context-aware practice.

Instructions

- Use in supervision groups, trainings, or as solo journaling prompts.

- Shuffle and select 1–3 cards at the start or end of a session.

- Discuss: What emotions, insights, or discomfort does this raise?

- Each card includes a **Reflection Prompt**, a **Clinical Lens**, and an **Accountability Action**.

CARD 1: Housing Crisis & Mental Health

Reflection Prompt: What is my current housing situation, and how does it shape my assumptions about stability?

Clinical Lens: Have I pathologised a client's anxiety or "chaotic lifestyle" without acknowledging the trauma of housing insecurity, rising rents, or homelessness?

Accountability Action: Name housing stress explicitly in formulation. Ask: "What does home mean to you?"

CARD 2: Childcare and Carework Pressures

Reflection Prompt: Do I assume my clients have time or space to attend therapy uninterrupted?

Clinical Lens: Have I interpreted missed appointments or lack of engagement as resistance—when the client may be choosing between care duties and survival?

Accountability Action: Name unpaid care as labour. Be flexible in rescheduling and validate the emotional cost of caregiving.

CARD 3: Migration, Borders, and Documentation

Reflection Prompt: What does it mean that I do not worry about deportation or visa rejection?

Clinical Lens: Have I overlooked the psychological toll of immigration status, Direct Provision, or refugee precarity?

Accountability Action: Learn the basic structure of Ireland's asylum or residency system. Ask: "Do you feel safe interacting with institutions here?"

CARD 4: Medical & State Authority

Reflection Prompt: Do I assume institutions like the HSE, courts, or schools will act in my client's best interest?

Clinical Lens: Have I referred someone to a service without acknowledging how those systems may have failed or harmed them before?

Accountability Action: Co-create referrals. Ask the client: "Have you had good or difficult experiences with this kind of service in the past?"

CARD 5: Institutional Mistrust

Reflection Prompt: Have I ever felt unsafe or surveilled when engaging with public systems? If not, what does that say about my positionality?

Clinical Lens: Do I label client mistrust as paranoia or non-compliance?

Accountability Action: Acknowledge the legitimacy of mistrust: "Given your experience, it makes sense to feel cautious."

CARD 6: Language and Documentation

Reflection Prompt: How often do I question the language I use in reports or case notes?

Clinical Lens: Do I use terms like "non-compliant," "poor insight," or "resistant" without exploring cultural or systemic context?

Accountability Action: Invite the client to co-author descriptions when possible. Replace clinical shorthand with relational understanding.

CARD 7: Class & Resource Insecurity

Reflection Prompt: Have I ever had to skip meals to pay rent? Do I understand that survival is a full-time job?

Clinical Lens: Do I assume clients have disposable income for private services, transport, or childcare?

Accountability Action: Map out the financial demands therapy places on clients. Adjust expectations accordingly.

CARD 8: Neutrality and Silence as Harm

Reflection Prompt: Do I believe therapy should be "neutral" on politics, race, or inequality?

Clinical Lens: Has my silence about systemic injustice ever made a client feel unseen?

Accountability Action: Name structural trauma where appropriate. Say: "It sounds like this isn't just personal pain—it's part of something bigger."

Closing Use:

Invite practitioners to journal or discuss:

- Which card was the most challenging? Why?

- What is one small shift I can make in my practice this week?

- Facilitators may also use these as weekly check-ins or to guide case consultations from a decolonial lens.

Appendix 4: Discussion Guide: Decolonising Psychotherapy in Practice

This guide offers ten prompts for reflection and conversation, ideal for continuing professional development (CPD), supervision sessions, study groups, or peer learning circles. It invites practitioners to engage critically and personally with the book's ideas, and to apply them ethically within their own practice.

1. Whose knowledge do I privilege in my practice?

What theorists, traditions, or voices shaped your therapeutic training? Who was missing?

2. How do I understand neutrality in therapy?

Have you ever used neutrality to avoid political or cultural discomfort? What are the risks of silence?

3. What would a decolonised intake form look like?

How might you change your initial assessments or first-session language to better reflect clients' histories, identities, and collective wounds?

4. In what ways have I internalised colonial logics?

Do you ever pathologise behaviours that reflect resistance, communal survival, or spiritual practices? How might you unlearn this?

5. What is the role of the therapist in systems of power?

How do therapists participate in maintaining or disrupting institutional inequities—whether through education, diagnosis, or professional gatekeeping?

6. What cultural or spiritual practices do I draw from—and do I honour their origins?

Have you integrated tools (e.g., mindfulness, ritual, storytelling) without naming their lineage? How can you approach this more ethically?

7. What is my relationship to land, ancestry, and place?

How might reconnecting with your own cultural or ancestral lineage change your presence in the therapy room?

8. How do I care for myself while doing decolonial work?

What structures of collective support do you need to stay in this work without burnout, especially if you hold lived experience of marginalisation?

9. How can I use this book to shape institutional change?

Which concepts or chapters could inform training, policy review, or curriculum redesign in your setting?

10. What does humility look like in my learning?

When you are challenged or confronted, how do you respond? How do you remain open, curious, and accountable in your decolonial journey?

ABOUT THE AUTHOR

Talha AlAli, MSc, MA, is a Palestinian psychotherapist and founder of *Decolonised Minds*, a platform dedicated to decolonised, culturally grounded and politically conscious approaches to mental health. With nearly two decades of clinical and humanitarian experience, Talha has worked extensively with survivors of war, torture, and forced displacement across the Middle East, North Africa, Eastern Europe, and Ireland.

He began his career working with children and adults affected by war trauma in Palestine, including survivors of torture, and then he moved to Jordan, where he joined Médecins Sans Frontières (MSF). Over the years, he has held key roles with MSF in several conflict zones—including Libya, Ukraine, and Bangladesh—where he managed mental health teams, provided therapy, and led capacity-building efforts for local professionals. His work included supporting survivors in Libyan detention centres, offering psychological care for children in MSF's reconstructive surgery hospital in Jordan, and reaching war-affected communities in occupied eastern Ukraine. In Bangladesh, he worked with survivors of sexual and gender-based violence and children subjected to labour exploitation.

Now based in Ireland, besides his private practice, Talha works as a psychotherapist with the Irish Red Cross (as of October 2025), providing therapeutic support to survivors of trauma and forced displacement. He has also worked in homeless shelters and with unaccompanied minors seeking asylum.

Talha holds a BSc in Psychology and Counselling, a Master's in Community Mental Health, an MA in Psychology, and an MSc in Pluralistic Counselling and Psychotherapy. His work is grounded in trauma-informed, culturally responsive care and a deep commitment to social justice. *Decolonised Minds* reflects his dedication to reimagining psychotherapy through an ethical, political, and decolonial lens.

www.ingramcontent.com/pod-product-compliance
Lightning Source LLC
Chambersburg PA
CBHW051257020426
42333CB00026B/3246